Management of d

ENGINEERING MANAGEMENT

Series editor S. H. Wearne, BSc(Eng), PhD, CEng, FICE, Consultant, Director of Institution courses and in-company training

Editorial panel D. E. Neale, CEng, FICE; D. P Maguire, BSc, CEng, FICE; D. J. Ricketts, BSc; J. V. Tagg, CEng, FICE; J. C. Bircumshaw, CEng, MICE; G. D. Cottam, BSc, CEng, FICE

Other titles in the series

ENGINEERING MANAGEMENT

Management of design offices

Edited by
P. A. Rutter, MSc, DIC, CEng, FICE,
FIStructE, MConsE
A. S. Martin, MSc, CEng, FICE, FIHT, FBIM

Thomas Telford, London

Published by Thomas Telford Ltd, Thomas Telford House,
1 Heron Quay, London E14 9XF

First published 1990

British Library Cataloguing in Publication Data
  Rutter, P. A. and Martin, A. S.
  Management of design offices.
  1. Management. Techniques
  I. Title
  658.4

ISBN: 0 7277 1383 3

Typeset in Great Britain by MHL Typesetting Limited, Coventry
Printed and bound in Great Britain by Mackays of Chatham.

Preface

This guide has been written to help engineers and others to manage design offices effectively and efficiently: *effectively* employing people and their ideas, expertise and enthusiasm to produce the drawings, specifications and other information that define a project; and *efficiently* producing this information to agreed standards of quality and safety, in time and within budget.

Until recently it may have been assumed that the contents of this guide would be of more interest to those engaged in the private sector than in the public sector. It now seems that this will change in the near future. Local authority design offices, which have until now been organized on traditional lines, will change considerably if competition in the provision of professional services becomes compulsory. Even if this does not come about by government regulation, the general atmosphere of competition in the provision of services in local government, coupled with financial pressures to provide value for money, is likely to result in local authorities introducing competition into the provision of professional services without waiting to be compelled to do so.

To introduce the subject the guide starts with a chapter on design planning which reviews the steps involved, from initial proposals to project schemes, cost estimates, quality plans, construction sequences, contract documents, detailing and as-constructed records. Obtaining a comprehensive brief from the client is stressed as an essential requirement for successful progress through the stages from the inception of a project to the conclusion of construction.

Design is an iterative process, with every stage requiring both a check on compliance with the brief and monitoring of the expected construction cost. The programming of the design and drawing production and the establishment of a budget for design office costs are discussed, as is the application of monitoring techniques to control compliance with the programme and the office budget. The treatment of overhead costs is examined, the approach adopted varying with the type of organization.

The chapter concludes by emphasizing the need to provide quality of service, which the introduction of a quality system can help to achieve. In some offices this may require merely the formalization of procedures already firmly established; for others it may need a fundamental review of current procedures. Checking should be undertaken systematically and not introduced as an afterthought when errors in drawings or documents begin to be discovered on site. In particular, a review of the initial design should be undertaken to establish that the concepts are sound. The detection of an error in principle or lack of compliance with the client's brief in the initial design will prevent expensive changes at a later stage.

The chapter on organizational choices deals mainly with management of people. It considers the extent to which formal systems may be effective, the comparative advantages of project-based and discipline-based teams, effects on motivation and the need for mobility and for staff reviews, audits and development.

Starting with a review of the structure of organizations and how this differs with the size and type of work undertaken, the chapter considers the comparative advantages of deploying staff in either project-related or discipline-related groups. The former implies changes in the formation of the group from time to time as the project creates more or less demand for staff, whereas the latter produces a stable grouping. Each has its advantages. Mobility of staff gives more opportunity for an individual's capabilities to be assessed by a number of managers. A discipline-related grouping can, at its best, make it possible for a strong identity and team spirit to develop. Within the groups, relationships must be conducive to efficient working and to promoting a desire to progress projects with an awareness of the constraints of programme and budget.

With growth, an organization needs to undertake periodic reviews to ensure that management does not become remote from its staff. Sustaining the personal involvement of partners and directors at all levels within a growing firm may not be possible and may have to be replaced by a management style which can both direct staff efficiently and maintain the sense of participation in the development and well-being of the organization which is the attraction of a small firm. These concepts are also applicable to the individual employed in the department of a large public authority.

The subject of motivation is dealt with in this chapter together with the related need to provide job satisfaction. Opportunities must exist for people to demonstrate their capabilities, and a system of appraisal must allow top management to become aware of individual effort so that reward can be given and progression to higher grades can be achieved. The aspirations and expectations of staff differ from one individual to another, but there should for all grades of staff be a discernible career development path which is open to those with the requisite ability.

As the size of a firm or department increases, so the more important it becomes to achieve effective communication and delegation. Poor communications are not only annoying for staff but can also be damaging to the design or drawing productivity and may lead to abortive work. Above a certain size the design office or project design group cannot operate satisfactorily without a clear system of delegation. Reliance on one individual to control at all levels the activities of his team will lead to inefficiency in the team, and to a potential health problem for the individual.

The guide then describes, in successive chapters, four cases of managing design offices. The cases vary in size of organization, type and size of project, and whether the design office is operating as an independent consultancy or as a service department within client or contractor companies and authorities. The four chapters describing these cases have been developed from papers presented at a seminar held by the Institution of Civil Engineers. They show differences in the form and the extent of organizations, in their management systems and in leadership style. Readers are recommended to compare them, see how they illustrate the principles reviewed in the earlier chapters and assess what may be helpful for their own needs.

The final chapter of this guide is a commentary on developments in computer support to design, drafting and office management. The total field of computer applications is beyond the scope of this guide, but both the introduction of computers and the expansion of their use in the design office do require considerable attention to the management of those facilities. Although computer systems provide a means of improving output and quality, the transfer of large sections of a firm's work onto a computer requires considerable organizational control. Reliance upon the computing installation is thereby increased, as is the vulnerability of the organization to the effects of failure of the system. Good housekeeping with formal and systematic back-up of the files that have been generated is an essential safeguard which extends even to word processing.

The author of this chapter warns of the need to understand the limitations of software programs and the importance of verification, especially where analytical software is developed in-house by a specialist in a particular discipline and the program is not widely used by others. New programs should not be relied upon until there have been extensive checks on the output, corroborating the results with known solutions for a wide range of examples. Similarly, independent checks on the input and output data should be a standard procedure during everyday use of programs.

Although the size and nature of the work undertaken in design offices may differ from one organization to another, the objective to be achieved by efficient management is common to all: to complete the design task within the allotted time and budget.

Although parts of the content of this guide may already be familiar to the reader, it is hoped that sufficient knowledge will be gained to stimulate design organizations to consider their effectiveness and efficiency and to review their management techniques.

P. A. Rutter
Scott Wilson Kirkpatrick
London

Acknowledgements

The Authors are indebted to Brian Redknap, City Engineer of Coventry, for the design brief given in Appendix 1.1 and to Brian Raper, City Engineer of Leicester, for supplying Fig. 2.2

The Author of chapters 1 and 2 is very grateful to colleagues who took the trouble to read the draft text of one or both chapters and make helpful suggestions, namely Roger Hawkins, David Hudson, Vivian Payne, John Pike, Brian Raper and David Rogers.

Contents

1　Design planning

Introduction
Managing a design office successfully demands personal skills to enable one to motivate and control people as well as to organize communications between them, coupled with engineering experience to comprehend the needs of construction and foresee problems. A design office is a kind of production department and should be organized and managed as such. It is paid to produce the information needed to complete projects on time, to budget and to the satisfaction of the client, whether the design office is in-house or not.

The principal objective of design organizations, whether private or public, is to make a surplus of income over expenditure, i.e. a profit. When profitability is achieved and sustained, further desirable objectives can be pursued; time and effort can be expended on expanding the organization, venturing into new markets and developing new skills. Low profitability or, worse still, prolonged periods of loss lead to undue preoccupation by senior management in investigating the consequences of losses, increases in staff turnover because of lack of competitive salaries and a standstill in modernization of office systems and improvements in the working environment. Other activities, such as looking ahead and development, are curtailed. The organization must be profit driven, otherwise the resources will not be available to do the work it is capable of undertaking.

For a consulting practice, the design and drawing offices are where the profits or losses are made and where effort must be concentrated to control job costs. A contracting firm, while needing to attend to profitability at every stage of work on a project, may achieve a profit by increasing expenditure on design or research to obtain economies during construction. Nevertheless, there should still be careful control of design office expenditure to allow the job to be constructed within the tendered sum.

For an organization to achieve its targeted profitability in a financial year, a budget should be established for the period, identifying the outgoing expenditure entailed in running it. Irrespective of the size and nature of an organization, the major expenditure in the design office is on staff salaries, typically two-thirds of the total costs. It follows, therefore, that for projects where the fees are not time based, the profit principally arises from completing the design work in the minimum time commensurate with fulfilling satisfactorily the assigned task.

In managing a design office it is worth recalling the truism that the whole is the sum of the parts; this is particularly appropriate in offices undertaking a large number of jobs of different size. There is no success for the organization that concentrates on making large projects profitable, only to see these gains overtaken by the losses incurred on the numerous small jobs which pass through the office almost unnoticed. To guard against this happening, it is essential to budget for every job, to set targets for staff to aim for and to monitor regularly the expenditure of time on the project.

It should be noted that in setting targets for staff there must be an expectation that often budgets will be exceeded, sometimes owing to extraneous circumstances, and therefore a contingency item must be allowed to enable the desired profit to be achieved.

What other steps can be taken to safeguard profitability? Depending on the type of commission being undertaken, some or all of the following safeguards can be introduced.

- Define the task clearly at the time of tendering or entering into a fee agreement.
- Use historical costing with allowances for inflation and wage increases to arrive at job cost budgets.
- Match the fee quoted to the quality of the design required by the client.
- Choose the right calibre of staff for the job.
- Undertake the various stages of the design at the appropriate time — not too early, not too late.
- Monitor and control the man-hours expended from the start of work on each project, as well as throughout all stages of

the work — do not wait until the job becomes a financial disaster.

- Remove staff from the project when the programme is delayed.
- Control the non-recoverable expenses by regularly monitoring them against the job budget.
- Seek additional fees before embarking on design alterations requested by the client.
- Improve design office techniques to minimize staff costs — examine the benefits of investment in computing hardware and software.

In-house and consulting design offices
Design offices are of two main types, i.e.

- in-house offices which provide a continuing service to the organization as a whole, for example in a public authority or large contractor
- consulting engineers who are commissioned to provide a design, either one-off for a specific project or purpose or working with regular clients in a manner very similar to in-house offices.

In chapters 3—6 of this guide there are examples of the way in which these two types of design office are organized to undertake projects of various sizes and complexity.

Roles and responsibilities
An in-house design office encompasses the two roles of representing the client who commissions projects and a service undertaking the work. To perform both roles satisfactorily the two should be clearly separated, for instance by being considered as independent cost centres.

A firm of consulting engineers should have its own objectives, of which the following are examples.

- To aspire as an enterprise to attain high standards of integrity and quality.
- To provide efficient and effective consultancy services in construction to all clients at all times.
- To provide sufficient funds annually for growth and development of individuals and the enterprise.
- To provide a secure working environment for all employees.

3

The design process in construction is usually for individual projects, each one being different from the other, although there may be much in common between them, be they structures, highways, bridges or pumping stations. Over time each design office will have developed its own preferred practices based on its successes and failures. It should draw on experience as well as current standards and codes of practice when evolving designs for new schemes.

Managing the design process

Design is a creative activity which can be very interesting to those employed in it, but tensions can easily arise if new ideas and solutions appear to be rejected without proper consideration by senior staff. Thus managing design staff calls for particular skills, including diplomacy and tact.

The way in which design is organized should be affected by the size of the project, the time-scale and the number of staff engaged upon it, but in essence the steps to be gone through are always the same and are shown in Fig. 1.1.

Obtain client's brief and budget

Arrange site investigation

Make feasibility study

Draft programme

Survey site

Conceive alternatives, including estimates of cost

Preliminary design

Select preferred scheme

Detailed design

Seek statutory approvals

Prepare contract documents

Obtain tenders

Supervise construction

Write operating and maintenance guides

Test and commission

Prepare records as-built

Review design

Monitor maintenance

Fig. 1.1. The design process

For all projects the essential requirement is a brief from the client defining the purpose of the design and the objectives to be met in both specific and qualitative terms. The brief may include items such as manning levels for operating and maintaining plant and whether the project is to be capable of being remotely controlled (for example a pumping station), the scope for using combined heat and power, and energy consumption limits where appropriate. An example of a design brief for certain highway structures is given in Appendix 1.1.

The completeness of the client's brief will depend on the amount of preliminary work that has been done. If no work has been done at all, the brief for a highway scheme, for example, may require a feasibility study, a site investigation, a land survey and the preparation of alternative lines; if, however, the preferred line has been chosen, the brief will refer to matters of detail. For a pumping station the brief may specify the capacity of the pumping plant in detail, leaving everything else (for example whether to have wet or dry wells) to the designer to propose alternatives.

It is the task of the designated group leader to formulate a programme to produce the design to meet the objectives within the time-scale laid down. The details of his programme should be agreed with his supervisor as well as with members of his team, all of whom need to be committed to the programme if it is to succeed.

Conception

Large structures, whether bridges, buildings or highways, are expensive to design and construct and so need to be satisfactory first time since there is little scope for modification once completed.

In formulating a concept for the scheme the individual designer of a small project, and the team for a large one, should draw on experience of similar work and also on the preferred solutions adopted in the particular office. At this stage the overall concept will be general and should allow for alternatives, leading to preliminary designs being prepared. Deciding the final design too soon may lead to the elimination of possibly better alternatives. On the other hand, not deciding soon enough and within the programme can result in wasted effort and dissatisfied staff. It should also be borne in mind that the cost of making changes at a later date can be high. Ideally, therefore, alternatives should be

5

considered as early as possible, taking all reasonable possibilities into account and having gained the commitment of the team and the client to the selected scheme.

In proceeding to the detailed design, account should be taken of any problems that have occurred in previous similar projects. Therefore a system for analysing both good and weak aspects of previous designs for similar problems should be well established and easily accessible in the office.

Design

Projects to be designed vary in size and complexity from motorways to junction improvements, from water reclamation works to small drainage works and from power stations to substations. A large project will be designed under a designated group leader, whereas a small one can be designed and managed by one person. Design offices vary in size and capacity. The scale of work that can be undertaken will depend on the size, capacity and experience of the staff. The *NCE consultants file 1989*[1] shows that the largest firm employs over 4,000 staff and the smallest 35, with a median of 131.

Design is mainly an iterative process as different ideas and solutions to each problem are considered, perhaps in discussion with colleagues, and some tried out on the board or screen. In *Principles of engineering organization*[2] S. H. Wearne defines three steps in making decisions on design: the first consists of defining the problem and the criteria for solving it; the second is to evolve alternative solutions; and the third is to analyse and evaluate those alternatives. If no solution satisfies the requirements the cycle should be repeated. These three steps are shown in the rectangles in the middle of Fig. 1.2, which is derived from Wearne. The experienced designer follows this process intuitively, but deliberate use of such a model may help the leader of complex design work to plan action to resolve a critical problem.

Designing may be done with pencil and paper on a board, or using a sophisticated single- or double-screen workstation running a drafting program. For all but the smallest highway schemes, for example, the terrain modelling would be done on a computer using survey data and established criteria for horizontal and vertical curves. Whatever method is used, the ultimate aim is the same: namely to produce drawings whose purpose is to give clear and

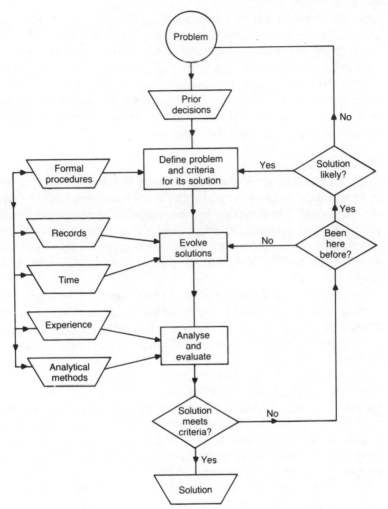

Fig. 1.2. Formal steps in making a design decision

unambiguous instructions to the recipient, bearing in mind appropriate standards, including British Standards, codes of practice and specifications such as the Department of Transport specifications.

It has always been an advantage for some projects to be produced in model form, and this can be done quickly and frequently using a three-dimensional computer-aided design (CAD) program that can show, for example, terrain modelling, the exterior of buildings from various points of view and also the interior of buildings. This latter facility can be particularly useful in examining complex service pipe runs.

Regarding major projects, regular progress meetings with all those involved are needed to examine all aspects of the design to ensure that the necessary co-ordination of the different parts of the project is being properly undertaken.

Checking designs

All designs should be checked to ensure freedom from error by an independent engineer or team who may be employed in the firm or department. The checking procedures should be clearly defined and their implementation monitored. The procedures should embrace a review of the assumptions, standards and design methods adopted, as well as the routine checking of calculations and drawings.

Design reviews and checking should be undertaken by engineers more senior or more experienced than the designers. Clearly work already done should not be repeated, but selective checking by an experienced engineer should highlight any error or questionable decisions.

The absence of checking procedures or failure to follow an established system could lead to a prosecution against the firm or persons involved if a disaster, large or small, resulted from errors in an unchecked design or drawing. For certain types of projects such as major bridgeworks, large structural falsework or reservoirs, there are statutory requirements for independent assessment of the designs by an engineer external to the firm.

It is neither necessary nor desirable for the checking to await the completion of the design: the design and the checking can be carried out together, it being desirable that there is agreement, or resolution of differences, as work proceeds.

Calculations should be set out clearly so as to be readily understood by other engineers. The calculation sheets (and computer print-outs where appropriate) should be referenced so that they can be related to diagrams of the relevant parts of the project. Checking calculations should go beyond an arithmetical check and should include an assessment of design assumptions, preferably by a method analytically independent of that used by the designer and thus done without reference to his calculations, although in some instances the computer print-outs may be used.

Drawings

Drawings should be prepared in accordance with BS 1192 *Construction drawing practice*.[3] This standard is in four parts. Part 1 sets out general principles and is applicable to drawings produced by conventional means or by computer techniques, as well as to those to be reproduced using microfilming. It deals with the presentation of drawings, layout, scales, types of lines, projection systems, dimension lines, lettering and folding of prints. It describes different kinds of drawings, for various stages of work.

- *Preliminary drawings* convey a visual impression of the designer's interpretation of the brief, usually in orthographic projection and accompanied perhaps by a pictorial impression. They show the feasibility of a scheme on which an estimate of the order of costs can be based.
- *Production drawings* can include location drawings, layout drawings, assembly drawings and component range drawings and schedules. They are often used to accompany applications for statutory approvals and as contract drawings.
- *Record drawings* are often based on production drawings but incorporate a record of construction as-built and of services as-installed. They should show the location of all hidden components or services and underground and within-construction works, and they should facilitate the carrying out of maintenance, repair and alteration work.

The preparation of record drawings is much neglected. Failure to prepare up-to-date records of construction and subsequent changes can cause problems and increased costs in future years, for example in locating services. It could make the engineers responsible liable for criminal prosecution if their neglect affects health or safety.

Part 2 of BS 1192 illustrates the general principles that are given in Part 1 and the application of the symbols and conventions given in Part 3. Part 4 gives recommendations for the preparation of landscape drawings and schedules.

One of the more difficult and time-consuming aspects of drawing is lettering. A few people have a natural ability to letter well; most

9

do not. Using a CAD program removes the difficulty. Older alternatives are to use stencils or pre-formed letters. Lettering machines are available which produce words (for example titles or descriptions) on transparent strips that adhere to the drawing. Although initially expensive, they may cover their cost in time saved.

Planning

How and how much one plans design should depend upon project objectives (for instance the importance of speed relative to cost) and upon the complexity and uncertainty of the design work. Usually the programme should be based upon estimated times for each of the tasks shown in Fig. 1.1.

The completion date for a project should be determined by or in consultation with the client. For a commercial project required for manufacturing or retailing, achieving or bettering dates will be crucial in starting to generate future income. For a public sector project the completion date may be influenced more by the availability of capital funds as between one year and another, for which purpose the project may have to be phased over several years.

The programme for the design of a complex scheme or uncertain work should be produced in the form of a network. For large projects a hierarchy of programmes will be suitable for different levels of staff. A summary programme may be best for each project, together with a staff allocation programme, with a programme showing activities in detail for each design section or project team. There are several software programs available for use on microcomputers based on critical path analysis, many of which include facilities for resource smoothing.

Budgeting

The budget for design should be based on anticipated fee income, which will be related to the estimated cost of the scheme; or it may be based on man-hour costs for similar schemes previously completed. Estimated times for each task should be stated in man-hours, which will indicate the number of people required on each activity over the period planned in the programme.

The designated group leader will then be able to assess the requirements for staff for each task and plan for them to be available when needed to ensure the completion of each phase of the design process. Much of this planning work is made easier for complex schemes or a multiplicity of jobs by using resource allocation programs on a microcomputer.

It is important that all staff engaged on a project know the time schedules for each phase of the work so that those who have several jobs in hand at any one time can plan their own work accordingly. Each one needs to know when his or her work is to begin and end, and what is to precede it and follow it, so that they can see their work as part of the whole and understand the importance of their contribution.

When several groups or teams are involved in different aspects of a project, such as a feasibility study, a survey or structural analysis, it is important for the members to know where their work fits in to the whole scheme, and to understand that the times shown on the time-sheets that they complete or the data that they feed into the control programme will be charged against the project budget. For those engaged on a variety of schemes it may be necessary for work to be recorded in short intervals, which will mean completing time-sheets every day, whereas those engaged for long periods on one main activity can complete sheets less frequently.

Management style

In considering matters of time and costs, staff sometimes get the impression that management is concerned only with the quantity of output, while they themselves are more concerned with quality. Thus the need for information on time spent on different aspects of work, so as to control costs, should be fully understood by staff if their co-operation is to be forthcoming.

Ideally, timing should be such that there are no gaps when one team is waiting on the completion of work by another before being able to make its contribution, since this constitutes delay. Equally, working hastily to complete by a deadline should be avoided as this can lead to errors and to employee dissatisfaction. All this means that information on programmes should be widely and openly available, and discussion by staff of the problems of achieving target dates should be encouraged so that solutions can be found by those immediately involved.

It is inevitable that the most carefully planned time schedules will be upset by delays of one kind or another, caused by matters

11

such as lack of information, hesitant decision making by other parties, breakdown of equipment and staff absences. Therefore, to allow for contingencies, programmed completion dates should be at least 20% earlier than needed.

Staff may complain that planning is a waste of time because no job ever runs to time, but this is to take a narrow view. Without an overall plan into which each major activity is fitted, all activities would follow sequentially, and there would be delays between the completion of one task and the commencement of the next. Final completion would come when it may. Although there are some jobs in which this would be acceptable, most have to be completed in a predetermined time in order to satisfy a client. The resources of the office will be under-utilized and the cost of the job increased if work is not planned so that each member is usefully employed all the time.

One problem that causes conflict is the time, and thus cost, that support staff allocate to a job. Overheads from central departments such as accountants, lawyers, administrators and typists are sometimes viewed by engineers as an unnecessary burden on their jobs. They sometimes are, and so it is very desirable that group leaders should specify which services they require, at what time and for how long and have a degree of control over the whole budget for a project.

Planning ahead also enables management to decide in advance when it will be able to take on more work and when that too is likely to be completed. The management may be responsible for many schemes of varying size and duration and will need to use control techniques to ensure not only that each project is on target, but also that all schemes are together capable of being carried out within the available resources, supplemented as necessary with temporary staff.

Monitoring and control

Administrative paperwork in design offices should be kept to a minimum as most engineers dislike it, seeing it as a diversion from the real tasks of thinking, deciding and designing. However, some paperwork is essential for monitoring and control and for future estimating. Its purpose and relevance should therefore be understood and accepted by everyone involved, and should be reviewed from time to time to ensure its continuing worth.

At the outset, a project brief that describes the objective should be reproduced for the groups or sections involved. Accompanying it will be a statement saying how the work is to be organized within the department and giving the programme, including stage completion dates, and budget. To be effective, progress needs to be monitored regularly by group leaders and the results discussed with the staff. Summaries to be used for control and monitoring should normally be produced weekly and made available to all interested parties as soon as possible. Updating programmes, whether on charts or computers, is only as accurate as the information fed into the system by staff who too often feel that the time spent in completing forms is wasted as they receive no feedback. They therefore feel little incentive to make returns accurate and fully representative of the work on which they are engaged.

There may be key dates in the programme (sometimes called milestones) by which it is planned that certain activities should be completed. Progress towards milestones needs to be examined with particular care. If delays at one such stage are not expected to be absorbed by savings in time at future stages, then the programme should be adjusted, or more resources should be allocated to the project.

The manner and extent of control should also depend upon objectives and needs. If work is late or too costly or if its completion is uncertain, the remedy may not be the obvious one of adding more monitoring and control. These actions add to cost, reduce designers' productive time and can demotivate designers and everyone involved. The problems may be occurring because of a lack of realistic or detailed planning, because of poor leadership or because of too much leadership.

There are as yet no statistical guides to deciding how much effort to employ in planning, leadership, monitoring and control, as the work of design offices varies so much in its complexity and novelty, the culture and experience of staff and the uncertainties of clients' objectives. Needs also tend to change from stage to stage of each project. One general principle is that detailed planning is rarely wasted, as it helps to anticipate problems. If in doubt, control should be reduced. To judge, symptoms are a guide. For instance, if workloads are erratic, budgets are not available, priorities are changed frequently and unexpected meetings are called to discuss these problems but they all recur, it is likely that there is too little planning, too much control and a lack of attention to how the senior managers are using their own time.

Reviews

Reviewing a completed project in whole or in part can be an effective means of learning from, and analysing the causes of, problems with a view to avoiding them in the future. It is one means of seeking better solutions to familiar problems. As well as appraising the design for effectiveness and cost, problems of construction should be considered.

Reviews are time consuming, since to be of use they must be thorough. However, time spent in a review should result in better solutions, with improved quality and lower costs of both design and construction of future schemes.

Annual budget

For a firm to survive, its income must at least cover all its costs and should provide a surplus to finance growth. A percentage must be added to the cost of salaries to cover overheads, including rent and rates, insurance premiums, equipment and training. This on-cost can vary from 50% to over 150%. Allowance has to be made for training, holidays and sickness; typically this may be based on around 85% of the paid hours being productive and may be covered in the on-cost.

An annual budget will give a forecast of work to be undertaken in the forthcoming year. It may include objectives for each manager which would be reviewed periodically in discussion with the head of department or partners. Monthly monitoring of income and expenditure, and of productive time per individual, is needed to ensure that the budget is being adhered to and to allow for adjustments to be made as necessary. Although more work is now being offered on the basis of fee competition (which may be a lump sum, an hourly rate or a percentage of standard fee scales), many clients are more concerned with quality than the cost of fees, which after all are but a small part of the total cost of a project.

Allowance should be made for training for both qualified staff and those still under training agreements. Continuing professional development (CPD), or continuing education and training (CET) as the Engineering Council names it, is likely to play an ever greater

14

part in keeping staff up to date, especially when quality management systems become well established in construction.

Professional liability

The Consumer Protection Act 1987 increases the safeguards for consumers by, among other things, rendering those involved in making and supplying products potentially liable for damage caused by defective products. The provisions of the Act may apply to the construction industry, and it is important that systems for design and checking are adequate.

Although in the nature of things it is not possible to achieve perfection in design and construction, engineers are responsible for their designs, and when things go wrong a client may be motivated to seek recompense which may be available by recourse to law. However, it is usually necessary to prove negligence, which may be both costly and difficult. Even so, it is becoming increasingly expensive to obtain insurance cover for the risks involved. The Latent Damage Act 1986 attempts to rationalize liability for England and Wales, and the Law Commission for Scotland has the matter under consideration. The subject is dealt with in *Professional liability*.[4]

Quality systems

There is increasing discussion on quality in construction following the publication of the revised BS 5750.[5] It seems likely that the use of quality systems will extend from those very large projects in which BS 5750 has previously been used to a wider range of jobs. At its heart is the establishment of a quality management system (QMS) in the design office.

BS 5750 reminds us that a principal factor in the performance of an organization is the quality of its products or services. There is a worldwide trend towards more stringent customer expectations with regard to quality. Accompanying this trend has been a growing realization that continual improvements in quality are often necessary to achieve and sustain good economic performance. BS 5750 goes on to say that to be successful an organization must offer products and services that

- meet a well-defined need, use or purpose
- satisfy customers' expectations

15

- comply with applicable standards and specifications
- comply with statutory (and other) requirements of society
- are made available, at competitive prices
- are provided at a cost which will yield a profit.

BS 5750 says that to meet its objectives a company should organize itself in such a way that the technical, administrative and human factors affecting the quality of its products and services will be under control. All such control should be oriented towards reduction, elimination and, most importantly, prevention of quality deficiencies.

A QMS should be developed and implemented for the purposes of accomplishing the objectives set out in the firm's quality policies. To achieve maximum effectiveness and to satisfy customer expectations, it is essential that the QMS be appropriate to the type of activity and to the product or service being offered. A well-designed QMS is a valuable management tool in the optimization and control of quality in relation to risk, cost and benefit considerations.

Regarding design, management should ensure that all those who contribute to design are aware of their responsibilities for achieving quality. The design and verification activities should be planned and assigned to qualified personnel who are equipped with adequate resources. At the conclusion of each phase of design development, a formal, documented, systematic and critical review of the design results should be conducted. This should be distinguished from a project progress meeting, which is primarily concerned with time and cost.

On records, BS 5750 states that the system should require that sufficient records are maintained to demonstrate achievement of the required quality and to verify effective operation of the QMS.

Firms may apply to be registered with BSI as Firms of Assessed Capability; if they are successful this enables them to show that they have been satisfactorily assessed for the standard of their quality management systems.

Eurocodes and standards

There are several Eurocodes in preparation which will cover the design rules for most types of structure. They are intended to remove complications that are created by having different rules in the European Community member states, and they should improve the competitive position of the industry outside the European Community as well as inside it. The input to draft codes and standards is made by the BSI on behalf of the UK. In due time the national codes and standards of member states will be replaced by the European ones. It should soon be easier for UK consultants to gain local approval for designs to be used in other member states by using Eurocodes and standards.

Library

Most engineers keep a collection of information which they hope will be useful in their work. It consists of books, tables of data, standards of various types, specifications and reports. Some of this material will be out of date and it is unlikely to be comprehensive. Although individuals should be encouraged to collect useful information, one should not rely on them to keep and know the contents of all relevant publications.

All design offices should therefore include or have access to a library or information source containing all the material needed on a day-to-day basis. Several copies of some publications may be needed. The expertise of a professional librarian should be used to locate publications which are not available in the office library and which are required only infrequently so that they can be accessed promptly. For example, certain large libraries, listed in *BSI standards catalogue*,[6] hold a complete set of British Standards.

Project records

Records of completed jobs can be kept on microfilm or microfiche for ready access, since loose drawings tend to become separated from a set or damaged with frequent use. The existence of standard drawings should be known to staff to avoid duplication of effort. Each job should have its own file that contains not only record drawings of the project as-built, but also the structural calculations and copies of the site investigation reports, together with all other relevant papers.

Appendix 1.1. Design brief for highway structures: Foleshill— Holbrooks bypass, Rowleys Green to Lockhurst Lane section

1. Scope of Works

   The works comprise two highway bridges carrying the Foleshill— Holbrooks By-Pass over the Coventry to Nuneaton railway line, one highway bridge carrying Lythalls Lane over the Foleshill— Holbrooks By-Pass and three retaining walls.

2. Information Provided

   The following information is included to give general details of the works content:

Drawing No	Title
	1/50 000 Location Plan
	1/1250 Scheme Plan
181/10/1S/1P	GA Bedlam Lane Tunnel and Retaining Walls
181/10/2S/1P	GA Lythalls Lane Bridge
181/10/3S/1P	GA Three Spires Bridge
181/10/4S/1P	GA Bartlett Retaining Wall
Soil Report [part] by Exploration Associates Nov 1973	Site Investigation No S805
Additional Soil Report by WMCC Sept '85	Site Investigation No 1339/DB
Mining Report [part]	

3. Programme

   The design programme for the bridges is as follows:
   Design start   April 1987
   Design complete   March 1988

4. Objective

   The designer is required to provide professional services in accordance with the 'Association of Consulting Engineers

Conditions of Engagement 1981 Agreement 2 for Civil, Mechanical and Electrical Work and for Structural Engineering Work where an Architect is not appointed by the Client', as amended by the following:

6.1 Design Stage I

The following clauses shall be added:

[g] Providing Form TA1 in accordance with the Department of Transport Departmental Standard BD2/79 and any subsequent revisions for the approval of the City Engineer.

6.2 Design Stage II

The following clauses shall be added:

[e] Providing the City Engineer with a programme, monitoring and reporting progress on a monthly basis.

[f] Providing the City Engineer with a cost estimate of the structures.

[g] Providing the City Engineer with a design certificate and a check certificate in accordance with the Department of Transport Departmental Standard BD2/79 and any subsequent revisions.

[h] Advising the City Engineer on the need for special inspection or testing.

[j] Preparing bar bending schedules.

[k] Delivering to the City Engineer on completion of Design Stages I and II all calculations, drawings, records and maintenance manuals as are necessary to enable the City Engineer to construct and maintain the Works.

6.3 Construction Stage

The normal service during the construction stage, as described in Clause 6.3, shall be replaced by all or any of the following services as may be necessary:

[a] Advising the City Engineer on the appointment of site staff in accordance with Clause 8.

[b] Preparing any further designs and drawings which may be necessary.

[c] Examining the Contractor's proposals.

19

[d] Making such visits to site as the Consulting Engineer shall consider necessary to satisfy himself as to the performance of any site staff appointed pursuant to Clause 8, and to satisfy himself that the Works are executed generally according to the contract and otherwise in accordance with good engineering practice.

[e] Performing any services which the Consulting Engineer may be required to carry out under any contract for the execution of the Works, including where appropriate the supervision of any specified tests and of the commissioning of the Works, provided that the Consulting Engineer may decline to perform any services specified in a contract, the terms of which have not initially been approved by the Consulting Engineer.

5. Specified Requirements

[a] The carriageway loading shall be HA checked for 45 units of HB loading.

[b] The highway bridges are proposed to be category II structures under the requirements of the Department of Transport Departmental Standard BD2/79.

[c] The design must comply with Schedule TAS (December 1983) A, in Appendix A of the Department of Transport Departmental Standard BD2/79.

[d] Construction work to be in accordance with the DTp Specification for Highway Works 1986 and with the City Engineer's amendments and additions.

[e] Provide all specifications, quantities and such information that is necessary to construct the works for inclusion in the contract documents to be prepared by the City Engineer.

6. Additional Information

[a] The Foleshill–Holbrooks By-Pass is being designed by the City of Coventry, City Engineer's Department.

[b] Additional boreholes and an updated report are to be obtained in April 1987 by the City Engineer.

[c] The site investigation by Exploration Associates was undertaken in 1973. It was based on the then current proposals and contains references to the scheme which are no longer applicable. Since its preparation there has been

mining with subsequent settlement, therefore any levels should be considered carefully.

[d] British Rail are considering the possibility of reducing the line to single track and thus reducing the span of the two rail bridges.

[e] Confirmation of the British Rail intentions to remove the two sidings at Three Spires Bridge is expected in the near future.

[f] British Rail are currently preparing a long section of existing rail levels and their relevelling proposals, for the calculation of clearance.

[g] It is required to maintain single line traffic at Lythalls Lane. This may require the provision of a temporary bridge over the railway to the North of Lythalls Lane.

7. Submission of Tender

[a] The Consultant shall submit his tender on a Memorandum of Agreement (ACE Condition of Engagement 1981 — Agreement 2).

They must complete the following:

Article 4(a) for Class D work
Article 5
Article 6
Article 7

[b] The Coventry City Engineer's estimate for the works is £2 M and the tender should be based upon this figure.

[c] Computing costs shall be included in the design fee.

MINING REPORT

The Coal Board have previously removed some of the coal from beneath the site.

There is coal remaining at about 500m depth but the Coal Board have no plans at present for its removal.

The effect of its removal will depend on the method and direction of extraction.

The structures should be designed with this in mind.

2 Organizational choices

Organizational culture

The most appropriate type of organization for a firm or the department of a public body depends on the kind of work it does and its objectives. Forms of organization extend from the formal type with its emphasis on structure, rules and procedures, to the informal type composed of a loose grouping of individuals and having few rules. Whatever type is used, an organization should be a dynamic organism that changes to meet new demands and circumstances.

A formal type of organization is necessary where large numbers of people are employed so as to provide the means of communication for ensuring that objectives and policies are implemented, that jobs are fairly remunerated and that standards of service are given equally to all customers or recipients. Informal types of organization are most suitable where the work is innovative, and where ideas and concepts that are best evolved by individuals or small groups predominate. In all organizations there should be a mixture of the formal and the informal according to the work being done; for example, innovation is quite different from administration and demands a less formal style.

As the examples presented in this guide show, every design office will have a culture of its own, with formality necessary for things such as finance and administration, whereas the main creative work thrives best in a less formal environment. In the private sector, for example, much of the work is likely to be undertaken with little advance notice, and so teams or groups are formed quickly to do a job and then disbanded.

Few people have the opportunity to create a new organization; most organizations expand as work increases and are modified in incremental changes over time, with the result that it may become necessary at some time to review an organization as a whole to see if any major changes are desirable. Except for the smallest office, there is usually an organization chart which shows the hierarchy, i.e. lines of authority and relationships between posts. However, a chart is only two dimensional and therefore is unable to reflect the dynamic nature of the organization, the many inter-relationships between people and the hustle and bustle of day-to-day activity. Fig. 2.1 shows a typical structure for a firm of consulting engineers in which each partner or director would be responsible for one or more sections, and, if less formally structured, for one or more projects. Fig. 2.2 shows a typical City Engineer's department.

In all offices the work should be allocated on the basis of the competence of people at each level. Generally speaking, the larger and more abstract decisions are made at higher levels, planning decisions at middle levels, and detailed design decisions at lower levels. In effect this is hierarchical decision making, with delegation to the lowest level capable of deciding matters appropriate to the work. It is found in all organizations, although it is not always formally authorized. Care needs to be taken in allocating work by levels to see that people are encouraged to make the best use of their talents for their own satisfaction and for the benefit of the organization. Generally speaking, the fewer the levels, the more people will be involved in varied work, have more responsibility and have greater job satisfaction.

Inter-relationships in an organization can be complex and not always satisfactory even in the best run firm or department; not everyone has a sense of humour or is polite and considerate all of the time. There is also a natural tendency to defend one's own interests. This is not necessarily bad for the organization, as it is the organization which defines job descriptions, unless it conflicts with the need for it to be capable of handling unexpected problems, opportunities and ideas.

Groups

Design work can be allocated within an organization in different ways. It is usually undertaken by teams or groups of engineers and supporting staff, although individuals will design small projects and parts of larger ones. Groups may be formal — a project team, a section or a committee; or they may be informal — the squash players or a lunch group. Most people prefer working in groups

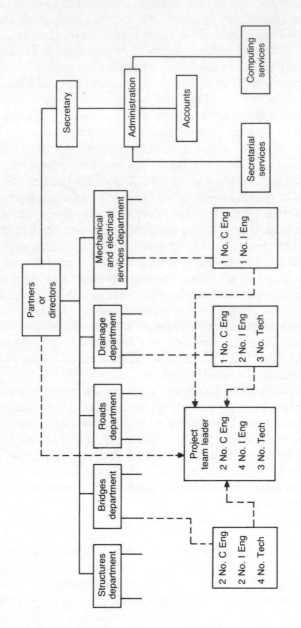

Fig. 2.1. Typical organization chart for a firm of consulting engineers

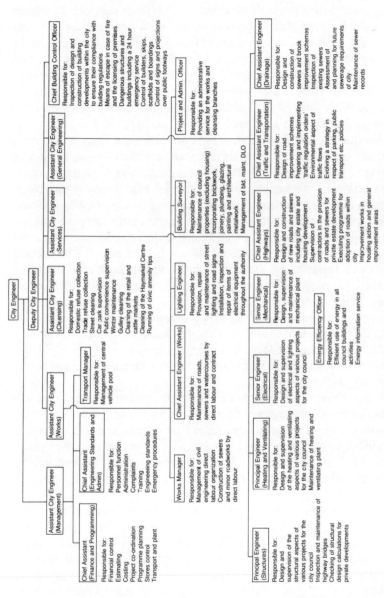

Fig. 2.2. Structure and functions of a typical City Engineer's department

as it satisfies their social and affiliation needs at work, facilitates the discussion of problems and generally affords support. Members of a work group should be compatible with one another in terms of skills, abilities, knowledge, ideas and outlook. Groups should be balanced in the proportion of senior to junior engineers and technicians, and work undertaken by everyone should be consistent with their skills. The size of a group can be important in maintaining interest and satisfaction — small yet adequate for the task in hand, with an upper limit of perhaps 20 people.

Frequently work groups, teams or sections are organized on a subject basis, whereby each group concentrates on one subject of design, for example on structures, highways, drainage, coast protection or mechanical and electrical services. Many engineers derive most satisfaction from specializing in a particular subject; they can become expert in it, can more easily keep abreast of developments and are quick and reliable decision makers. Younger members of a group organized on a subject basis can be trained by more experienced staff so that the group is able to maintain within its ranks a sound body of knowledge and experience. However, groups specializing in a subject may develop independence such that in large organizations it may become difficult to integrate their work with that of other subject groups in the furtherance of large and complex projects. There could also be problems from a lack of continuity if the demand for a particular subject slackens off.

Many projects are designed by multi-disciplinary groups of people who have complementary skills. Using such a group to undertake a whole project has the advantage that every expertise needed is available in the group, and this reduces problems of communication. If it is a permanent group, its members will be well known to each other, and their strengths and weaknesses understood.

In considering where to allocate a new project in the organization, it may be desirable to set up a special team or group drawn from its various parts. This is especially the case where the problem to be faced crosses the boundaries of specialisms or subject groups. One way of doing this is to use a matrix form of organization in which the project leader heads a group drawn from appropriate sections of the firm. While working in the group each member is responsible to the group (project) leader for his or her contribution to its work and to his or her normal superior (the functional head) for overall performance in that discipline. As each member's contribution is made he or she returns to his or her own section of the organization, and when the project is complete the group is disbanded.

Being a group leader calls for good inter-personal skills. He or she must be able to see clearly what needs to be done and must be able to lead the group to achieve it. The task of the leader of a matrix group is even more difficult as he or she must first mould the individual members together into a team, so that each one is able to make an effective contribution and time is not wasted on problems of communication or rivalry. However, it is easier to co-ordinate the work for a complex project involving several disciplines in one team than if it were being done by several subject groups. In addition the project leader may have to liaise directly with the client and other specialists inside and outside the organization.

Size

As an organization grows it has to be formed into sections of manageable size, with someone leading each section. More sections mean more levels, resulting in a pyramidical structure as illustrated in Fig. 2.1. Up to a point there will be economics of scale with growth, but beyond that point there are likely to be diseconomies, resulting in more time being spent on developing and maintaining systems of control and less on output. In any organization the proportion of support staff to design staff should be low.

A good administrative section will afford the necessary support to design staff in financial and legal matters, including terms of engagement, salaries, purchasing, monitoring the budget and maintaining the library. It relieves the engineers (whose task it is to maximize income without lowering standards) of routine work.

Increasing size brings problems of control of output and standards, together with problems of integrating work of different sections. This emphasizes the advantages of creating a work environment in which staff can use their initiative and where the amount of control and supervision needing to be exercised is at a minimum.

Management style

Managing creative engineers in a design office calls for knowledge and skill in managing people. The objective is to create an environment that will allow everyone to give of their best in their own way. Everyone in charge of a work group, team or section is a manager whose leadership and management skills either enhance or diminish the output of the group.

Group leaders, like all managers, derive their authority from two sources: their position in the organization and their personal qualities, and it is therefore desirable that the latter should support the former. If group leaders occupy positions above that which their personal qualities will support, they are unlikely to be very successful.

The style adopted by a manager will depend on a number of things, including personality, management knowledge and experience in handling people. Some managers naturally assume an authoritative style and expect their decisions to be implemented and instructions acted upon, and they often will be. It is a style which inexperienced managers are inclined to adopt, believing that it is their job to make the decisions, exert authority and generally to show that they are in charge. But for effectivness such a style depends on the potential to apply sanctions, which may include withholding benefits, including bonuses, and retarding promotion; it is not a recipe for a good working environment.

As work often has to be completed to strict limits of time and cost, this tends to instil into managers a high concern for output. It is also true that some managers, more concerned with good relations with their staff, show a bias towards maintaining those relationships even at the expense of output.

In any organization there will be short periods when output is so important that concern for people has to take second place, and staff will usually happily co-operate provided the situation is explained to them and it is not a regular occurrence stemming from mismanagement.

It is important at all times that staff are kept informed about their project and the organization's future, for example through team briefings. It is also important that they know the detail of production schedules for drawings and documents so that, as far as possible, their own work is not disturbed by unexpected events.

Motivation

The everyday task of all staff is to produce accurate work to proper standards, and as economically as is reasonably possible.

It should be seen as a team effort, with each member making his or her own contribution, and it is the job of managers — team leaders or group leaders — to try to maximize that contribution. To achieve that they must motivate their colleagues, usually by offering them a means of achieving their own personal aims, although they themselves may not be conscious of having particular aims. An individual's aims may be direct: to pass an examination, to create a new design solution to an old problem or to see a project through from beginning to end. Alternatively they may be indirect, for example to acquire material things and thus to work simply to increase spending power. A knowledge and understanding of people's potential needs will help everyone to think through their own desires and motivations as well as those of their colleagues, both senior and junior.

In setting out his well-known hierarchy of needs, A. H. Maslow suggested that a higher need was unlikely to emerge in a person until the lower needs were substantially satisfied. Maslow's hierarchy of needs is

- *physiological:* for example hunger and thirst
- *safety:* job security, protection from violence and crime, stability and order
- *love:* affection and belongingness
- *esteem:* self-respect, self-esteem, the esteem of others soundly based on real capacity and achievement, reputation and prestige
- *self-actualization:* the desire for self-fulfilment, to achieve all that one is capable of achieving.

Maslow tentatively suggested two other needs, which he believed may affect only people of relatively high intelligence: namely the desire to know, to satisfy one's curiosity; and the desire to understand, to analyse and to organize.

Managers should also know of the work of Frederick Herzberg, who evolved the motivation-hygiene concept. He described those factors which lead to job satisfaction as motivators. They are achievement, recognition of achievement, the intrinsic interest of the work, responsibility and advancement. Those factors which lead to a healthy work environment he described as hygiene factors. They are company policy and administrative practices, supervision, salary, inter-personal relations and working conditions. If dealt with properly, these factors serve primarily to prevent job dissatisfaction. There is much in common in the work of both Maslow and Herzberg, and these are but two of the many writers and thinkers on motivation.

It is for the management to see that the hygiene factors are dealt with satisfactorily in its policies and practices. It is the group leader's task to deal with other motivating factors, including recognition of achievement, responsibility, allocating work so as to stimulate interest, supervising with care and dealing with training and development within the overall policy of the organization.

Fundamental to motivating people successfully is the setting of goals or objectives, preferably in consultation with those involved. Individuals who are committed to goals are much more likely to strive to achieve them than if they are not committed; hence the need for consultation. If the achievement of agreed goals is to provide individuals with job satisfaction, they ought not to be too easily reached.

It is not always easy for staff to know the level of their performance in the context of the project as a whole, nor how it is viewed by senior staff. Hence another key factor in successful motivation is for staff to be kept informed of both the level of their performance as individuals within a project and their contribution to the organization as a whole.

Job satisfaction

Whatever general form the organization may take, it should not be static but should vary over time, during which one of its main purposes should be to provide an environment in which people can produce work of a high standard in a reasonable time. People who enjoy job satisfaction do not necessarily produce more, but the quality of their work and their application to it is likely to be good, and they are less likely to seek a move to another organization.

Matters which give rise to complaints by staff include

- arbitrary and inconsistent decisions
- lack of co-ordination of work
- an excess of paper work
- lack of delegation
- the unseen boss
- disturbance stemming from the need (in the public sector) to deal with enquiries from the public

- choices that are made (in the public sector) on the basis of political expediency rather than on objective criteria
- individuals who continue to work at the lower level after promotion, thus depriving others of the opportunity of undertaking that work, and at the same time failing to give leadership.

So far as possible, jobs should be designed to meet people's needs and thus make their work more satisfying. This should result in fewer absences, better quality of output and perhaps higher productivity and lower unit costs. Most people like to have plenty of interesting work to do, to organize it in their own way, to be free to take most decisions (and responsibility for them) and to feel that their efforts are appreciated and rewarded. Many also wish to develop their skills so as to be able to move up the hierarchy when the opportunity arises. Work can be made more interesting by job enlargement, i.e. by including a variety of work at the same level, or it can be enriched by giving individuals more responsibility for planning and organizing their work as well as for decision making.

It may be possible to deal with some of the complaints about day-to-day problems through the technique of management by objectives, particularly if it is not too formalized. Through discussion between senior and junior staff, it should be possible to clarify the extent of the work for which each person is responsible and agree a set of desired results or level of performance.

Delegation

Lack of delegation from their boss is a complaint that is frequently made by staff at all levels, but the full import of receiving it is not always understood or accepted, especially when things go wrong. In seeking more delegation some employees merely seek more freedom to act. They also need to be more willing to accept accountability for their actions. This suggests that staff are sometimes unclear about the extent to which they can act without approval to every detail. In these circumstances a clarification of roles may be all that is required, as much freedom as possible being given to staff at all levels.

Delegation is a specific act in which a senior person devolves some of his or her authority on to one or more of his or her junior colleagues, together with responsibility for the action which is subsequently taken. The limits of the delegation should be clear and well known to each of them. Although the juniors are responsible to the senior for what they do, the senior remains accountable to his or her superior for all the action taken in his or her name by the staff, and should not seek to avoid overall responsibility for their decisions and actions. It is a question of trust; delegation should be between people based on their abilities, not between posts, although job descriptions will set out the duties of a post, and the post-holder is expected to be capable of undertaking the level of work defined in it.

The span of control, or span of management of senior staff, has an effect on the amount of delegation needed: the larger the span the greater the need to delegate to subordinates.

Communication

Good communications are required to ensure that information – messages and instructions – is distributed to those who need it. Distribution is not sufficient in itself; messages are not completed until they are received and understood. They may be oral or written and communicated either to individuals or groups, depending on the kind of information and its purpose.

Much of the communication on design problems will be by discussion between senior and junior engineers or by peers rather than by the issuing of instructions. Short weekly or fortnightly meetings of team members are needed to identify delays and difficulties and to allow all members to contribute suggestions for improved solutions or working arrangements. This is not only valuable for the results themselves but also contributes to the generation of a good working environment and individual job satisfaction. It enables the team leader to develop communication skills, including listening, a desirable facet of managing that is often overlooked.

Procedure manuals

If similar events occur from time to time it is worth while preparing a written note so that on its next occurrence the matter can be dealt with as before without its having to be thought out again from scratch. Reducing the treatment of recurring events to systems also enables less senior staff to operate them. Numerous systems exist in offices, but if they are unwritten they are more difficult to learn and are subject to unconsidered incremental changes. Benefits that can accrue from a degree of uniformity in handling recurring matters are

- *better quality:* the experience of several people can be enlisted to devise a system for continuous use
- *economy:* staff are not involved in devising *ad hoc* methods as events arise.

Systems can be devised as the need arises and then become part of a manual of office procedures, which can be used for reference and for training new staff.

Training

Training is wanted by individuals to enable them to qualify in the first instance and later for career development; it is needed by the organization to replace staff who are promoted or who leave either for other employment or retirement. Training can very easily be a haphazard activity, but it ought to be planned on the basis of the needs of both the individuals and the organization. Some engineers will opt to remain in their subject area, while others will seek to gain management knowledge which should enable them to do their present work more effectively, whatever the level, and prepare them for advancement.

A formal system of continuing education and training (CET) as envisaged by the Engineering Council will make demands on both staff and employers as well as requiring adequate funding. Any scheme of CET should include the acquisition of management and business skills, not forgetting the increasing importance of having a foreign language.

Self-development by staff should be encouraged, and to this end they should gain experience in multi-disciplinary groups and also move between different specialist groups where appropriate, i.e. by job rotation. The broader their experience, the more capable staff should be of contributing to the work of project groups and eventually of managing a team or group themselves.

3 Design in a medium-sized consulting practice

The change in technology, together with competitive fee bidding and a stronger emphasis on legal responsibility, has forced today's design offices to address in greater detail the management of their offices. No longer can a profit be assured through the application of comfortable fee scales with further remuneration for extra services, as many traditional extras are now a necessary part of today's design solutions and are expected to be provided as part of modern design office procedure. The application of computers is perhaps the most obvious example of this change in working methods.

The estimating, planning and progress systems of a medium-sized (120 staff) consulting civil, structural and building services engineering practice is described against this background.

In today's world fee competition is common. Reference to historical records from similar projects for the time expended and the relationship of skills involved is beneficial in assessing the fee requirement. However, such statistics need to be modified when making projections, bearing in mind changing salary relationships; for example, technician remuneration has risen substantially in relation to that of more qualified staff in recent years. Overheads, and in particular professional indemnity insurance and social benefits to staff, are far more significant in today's costings.

In anticipating the future it can be assumed that competition will become more intense. Practices will need to be more aware of the true costs and economies that can be made, and those who do not respect the need to organize their management will be severely disadvantaged. If the foregoing is accepted then, drawing from the experience of the Author's practice, the following suggests a practical approach.

Organization

The practice is structured as a partnership whose partners choose first and foremost to be working engineers, with the predominance of their time devoted to the commissions of their clients. They use the services of professional advisors via solicitors and accountants but choose in principle to be in personal control of the managerial decisions of their business and therefore divide between each partner those necessary aspects of consultancy that do not directly relate to technical design.

Administration has always been a necessary aspect of the design process but not necessarily accorded the same value as design. Few architects or engineers have been trained to appreciate the principles of office management, and it is often surprising to find that they possess such little understanding of the standard forms of agreement upon which their office is appointed. All staff should be encouraged, to a greater or lesser degree, to make themselves fully aware of the contractual and financial implications of the projects on which they are working.

The scope of work, consequential responsibility and commercial exposure are as relevant to the continuance and growth of the business as is its ability to perform with technical competence and flair.

As organizations grow there is an acceptance that the administration department also grows, but increased size is not necessarily best served by merely increasing non-technical administrative staff. At a particular size there is probably a need to consider appointing a technical administrator whose background has been in the practice of the profession, and at the sharp end, yet who is equally motivated and able to oversee the business aspects of the office. Although accountants, solicitors and insurers can contribute valuable advice, they cannot fully understand the technical considerations nor translate their good advice when viewed from their professional viewpoint into the realities of the design profession. It is difficult for an accountant to support the substantial investment that is often involved in submitting for a project when success is not guaranteed, and when the firm came second in the two previous submissions. Similarly a solicitor must always advise that the firm should not start work let alone proceed to scheme stage without an agreed contract, although that is what many offices must do to ensure employment continuity with the client.

Accepting these views, the partnership has allocated individual partners to the following broadly-based tasks in addition to their specific project responsibility

- staffing, technical resources and training (staff partner)
- library, archiving and historical records (information partner)
- financial and legal matters (finance partner)
- project technical responsibility (all partners).

The practice is structured beyond the partners through associates, senior engineers, engineers, graduates and technicians. All are supported by technical and administrative staff responsible for the library, printing, archiving, accounting, communications and correspondence. More recently staff welfare and staff dining facilities have been separately provided for. Administrative tasks, both technical and non-technical, are delegated throughout the structure, thereby involving and making responsible all members of the practice in some way or other. Committees have been established to deal with all manner of necessary aspects of the business, including the maintenance of standard specifications, library needs, computer software requirements, the journal editorial board and in-house and external career training.

Commissions

Projects, be they by competition, enquiry or direct appointment, start their route through the practice via a POSSIBLE category, at which point a job number is allocated and the basic details are recorded with the financial section. The enquiry is reported at the next weekly partners' meeting and the appropriate project partner either confirmed or allocated the project responsibility.

Initial 'guesstimates' are made regarding the probability of award of the commission and the likely income that could be generated. The projected profitability of the potential commission is assessed. Initially this assessment is based upon 15–20% of the fee, and this provides guidance on the effect of the expenditure that should reasonably be committed to the enquiry if it is to remain profitable when successful yet not disproportionately costly if difficult. Clearly, established clients where regular commissions are generated should be served at a level different from that of new and untried contacts. Certainly substantial effort should not be embarked upon without the commitment of a client if the outcome is dependent upon the client's success when in competition with others for a project. Consideration should also be given to the influence the practice will have on the final outcome. For example, when helping contractors or developers on a no-job/no-fee basis, the designer may have no influence on the final bid price, however efficient the design solution may be, as that decision is often made without reference to the designer.

A budget for speculative expenditure having been established, regular monitoring of the costs being incurred is imperative. A monthly interval can be too long. Enthusiasm to serve a new client or win a competition is to be encouraged, but reality must hover in the background. Despite a weekly review, overspending against the target is not uncommon.

When it is apparent that a commission will be forthcoming, the form of contract, scope of service to be offered, fee required and invoicing stages are agreed between the project partner and the finance partner and are allocated according to the target work programme. These terms are communicated to the client. Upon receipt of the formal appointment the project is transferred to the ACTIVE category. Often work must start before the appointment is formalized, and care should be taken not to let the design advance too far before contractual matters are finalized. This is particularly important where time-based commissions are concerned. Hourly costs are expensive, and regular monthly billing accompanied by a very detailed scope of service provided is important to maintain client confidence and sometimes credibility. Clients often do not appreciate the significance of an engineer's effort in the preparation of design calculations because they do not normally see the pages of output.

The work plan

A work plan is established, and in doing so it should be appreciated that the standard terms of employment do not, as far as income is concerned, coincide with the rate of expenditure. They differ according to the particular profession, but generally architects tend to pre-fund the early stages of design to a greater extent than engineers, although architects' fees are ultimately likely to be more profitable than those of engineers. Care must be taken by engineers not to underspend in the early stages of the project, yet they must not assume invoiceable income to have been fully earned. The

Table 3.1. Typical percentage spend compared with invoiceable fees (ACE agreements)

Stage	Work effort: %	Invoiceable fee: %
Preliminary	7·5	15
Tender	25·0	45
Working drawing	50·0	25
Post-contract	17·5	15

typical percentage spend as compared with the invoiceable fees under Association of Consulting Engineers (ACE) agreements is shown in Table 3.1. In contrast the architects' method is to place a greater work emphasis, particularly in terms of final detailing, in the post-tender stage. This difference in work stage emphasis often results in changes or modifications to the completed work of an engineer. There is a need for a better understanding of the necessary working methods of engineers and architects.

The work plan is based on those parameters against which the job performance is to be monitored via the office data systems of invoicing, expenditure and time-sheets. The development of this plan starts with manpower planning. Partner time, senior staff time, engineers' and technicians' time are estimated in man-weeks. Average salary costs are applied to the time to arrive at an estimated drawing office salary cost. The project expenses, both recoverable and non-recoverable, are estimated, and the total income, including the recoverable expenses, is also predicted. These three estimates make it possible for the project projections to be made and, by using their equivalent actual figures (updated from time to time), for the project to be monitored.

Any system can only be as good as the quality and accuracy of the data on which it is based. All project staff are involved in assuring the validity of the data. The completion of time-sheets is perhaps the most contentious task within design offices. First, they must be accurate; hours casually booked, together with overheads etc., have a real effect on the projections, particularly for the smaller projects. Motivating staff to complete and hand in their time-sheets at a fixed time is a problem. Only by educating staff to a point whereby they subscribe to the need will this problem be overcome. It has been found that time-charged projects provide a useful avenue in the education process as all staff are, to some extent, involved in such work. A 'T' suffix to time-based jobs and a full description of the work undertaken, day by day, are required, and then the sheet is signed by the member of staff. At the point of preparation of the invoice the persistent offenders are invited to witness the process and observe how their own reluctance to adhere to the systems can cause them to be inoperative. Often the cause of their reluctance is a total lack of appreciation of the mechanics of the system and its relevance to the security of their own and the firm's future viability.

Estimating

The system of estimating and monitoring project progress described here may not be applicable to all offices. It is designed to be totally integrated with a computer system. The software is not commercially available and was written by the Author. The philosophy revolves around the minimum fundamental project records that most offices maintain: namely estimated and actual income, estimated and actual salary costs and estimated and actual project expenses.

Target recovery factor

If the estimated offsets are deducted from the estimated income the net income available for salary, overheads and profit is derived. If that net income is divided by the estimated drawing office salary cost (DOC), then a recovery factor (RF) based on salary cost is derived. If the number is 1 then nothing is available for overheads and profit, but as the RF increases a point is reached where a particular number, say $2 \cdot 4$, provides for the average overhead contribution necessary for the business to break even, i.e. overheads at, say, 140% of salaries. A higher factor than, say, $2 \cdot 4$ indicates that the commission will be profitable. The higher the RF the more profitable the commission.

Target profit (or loss)

At any time the total salary commitment of the practice is known and the total overheads can be estimated. A break-even recovery factor of total estimated overheads/total estimated salary can therefore be projected. Applying this to the financial target for the project gives the estimate of profit or loss as profit (loss) = net income × (target RF − break-even RF)

Cash flow and invoicing

The financial plan for each project is expressed on a month-by-month basis, with a cumulative total to date as far as expenditure is concerned. The fee which is to be invoiced according to contract stages and their timing is overplotted to give the resulting cash flow and probable pre-funding expectation. In this respect a time lag for payment beyond presentation of the invoice of six weeks is built into the equation. One constant problem for design offices is the size of the unpaid fee ledger. Designers pre-fund their clients at various stages of the design, and there must be a point at which late payment of invoices cannot be accepted. Interest can be provided for within agreements, but that is both difficult to enforce and no substitute for payment within a reasonable time. VAT output tax is worthy of consideration in this. All businesses are obliged to make payment to HM Customs and Excise at the appropriate time, irrespective of whether the invoice has been settled or not. It is prudent, therefore, to arrange the invoicing of substantial fees to be within the first month of the business VAT quarter to ensure the maximum time for payment before VAT liability becomes payable.

Monitoring

All staff complete time-sheets on a monthly basis, recording the times expended on each project against its respective number. These are costed at the close of the month and the total DOC for all staff in the month and the cumulative total to date are computed. Offsets in the form of expenditure via bank accounts, petty cash etc. are similarly computed on a job basis. Invoicing to that point is also computed. A further set of data are therefore available: the actual invoicing, actual offsets and actual DOC at that point. Progress can now be reported back to the project staff and considered by the project partner. If the cost of the time expended on a project is taken to be the determining factor then the current situation of any project is shown by

percentage complete = 100 × actual DOC/estimated DOC

earnings to date = (estimated income − estimated offsets)
        × percentage complete + actual offsets

future earnings = estimated income − earnings to date

cost to date = (actual DOC × break-even RF) + actual offsets

profit to date = actual DOC × (target RF − break-even RF)

fee cash flow = invoicing − earnings to date

With this information the position of the project can be considered. If, for example, the percentage complete is considered too high for the true progress of the project, then it follows that there is a need to reconsider the original estimate of manpower and increase both the staff allocation and therefore the estimated cost. If the income remains the same then it similarly follows that there will be a lowering of the target RF and a consequential reduction in profit. All other factors will also be varied.

As stated earlier, there is sometimes a need to monitor more frequently than monthly. However, it should only be the occasional job that needs such close attention. The greater emphasis will require a disproportionate amount of senior staff time and may lead to increased administrative staff, thereby increasing overheads and defeating the primary objective. If office project administration is to be taken seriously then the time incurred in undertaking this task by technical staff should also be budgeted for and monitored. A series of administration numbers can be allocated for these general tasks. The individual category and cumulative cost is monitored. Partners are not excluded from being part of this exercise and are expected to complete time-sheets. The basis of their cost is equated to that of senior staff by the allocation of notional salaries. A figure of approximately 4% of total practice time is found to be expended in the areas of project monitoring, staff interviewing and in-house committee work.

Computation

Most practices now have a desk-top computer dedicated to management tasks. Staff data, including salaries, make it possible for hourly costings to be computed, which with time-sheet information rapidly gives the total DOC. Data files of invoicing under job numbers as well as offsets from purchase data files are also readily available. The only non-factual information is that of estimating. This can only be done by those planning the job. This too may be held on a data file with other relevant job information. Appropriate software rapidly does the arithmetic and can sort according to partner, division, type of work etc. to produce reports to assist in the management decisions for each project.

Analysis

Obviously the individual job analysis is the first aspect to be considered, with amendments made in policy and projections where appropriate. However, having put into balance each project as best as one is able, a cumulative set of data combining all projects can be produced which, when combined with non-project data such as overhead costing, allow projections to be made for the business as a whole. Future workload and staffing needs can be predicted with a reasonable degree of accuracy, as can cash levels, profitability, and expansion/contraction.

Communication

Computers are most useful in compiling numerical data, but their output in numerical form tends to be extensive and difficult to absorb. By far the most interesting and comfortable output is that in graphical form. The use of pie diagrams and histograms is to be encouraged when large volumes of numerical data are to be communicated.

Historical data

In today's climate of fixed fees and competition between firms there is a clear advantage for those who understand their business and how to plan wisely at the start and then respond to events rapidly. On completion of a project it is useful to have the total hours expended by discipline, the cost, expenses, income, final recovery factor etc. filed separately, as well as information on the client, professional colleagues, location, scope of work, form of contract and so on.

Overheads

The recording of overheads has been found to be best separated under coded headings designed for computer analysis.

Conclusion

Design office systems are the key to successful management. It is not important what format they take provided that they communicate the necessary information and are reliable. Many engineers are not enthusiastic towards 'admin', this being seen by them as a task unrelated to their first love of being a designer. However, everyone can be properly motivated if the purpose of 'admin' is clearly understood and subscribed to as being relevant. To this end staff must be encouraged to learn the relevance of, and make suggestions for the improvement of, current systems. It is perhaps most important of all to ensure that they receive information regularly on the state of their projects and that they feel party to the assumptions, decisions and consequences of the task in which they are involved both technically and administratively.

4   Design in a large firm

Building and civil (B & C) design in British Nuclear Fuels plc (BNF plc) is carried out by the Works and Buildings (W & B) Department, a branch of the Company Engineering Division. The department comprises an integrated team of architectural, civil and structural engineers, 200 in number, which makes extensive use of external resources on a ratio of approximately 4:1, handling a capital workload of approximately £200 million per annum. The bulk of the work is of an industrial nature, is very complex and is closely integrated with nuclear process plant requirements.

Process requirements will normally dictate the size or scope of the B & C work, together with the need to link each new facility into the overall operations of the site by extending or connecting into an established infrastructure system. Historically, separate process facilities were linked by external pipe/service bridges and road and rail networks, and the individual sites were developed to meet the needs of a developing nuclear industry. More recently, however, much larger-scale complete process facilities have been planned to be more efficient in both development and operation and more economical in the use of land and infrastructure systems.

The complexity of the B & C work is dictated by the process or multi-process requirements of the plant or the requirement to design for extreme environmental events, usually by a combination of both. Generally these extreme events, wind, snow, rain and flood, and particularly seismic events, have significantly increased the complexity of analysis and design in recent years as more realistic methods have become available for assessing the loads and conditions to be sustained by the building.

44

Task definition process

The brief or scope of work required of the W & B team is established with the Project Office during the process of front-end design, the early design stage used to resolve the chemical processes and engineering systems. This front-end design culminates in a capital expenditure proposal to the Board and, in the process, defines a project brief for the W & B team, which includes

- the scale and type of design work involved – with a detailed assessment of the capital expenditure
- the responsibility required of the design team
- the complexity of the work, particularly with regard to analysis and design criteria
- the level of detail drawing work
- the level of quality assurance, and an indication of the parts of the work over which it is to apply
- time-scales for research and development, design/detail and construction/commissioning, which must be realistic.

Standard lists of information required for various stages of each project are used to ensure that proper attention is given to assessing the scope and complexity of the work at each stage, through concepts, cost estimates, preliminary designs, tender designs and finally working drawing stage design. The level of information required at each stage becomes increasingly more detailed to satisfy commercial, design and licensing requirements.

Design programming

Most of BNF plc's projects require detailed design team programmes to ensure that the necessary sequence, pace and progress of the work is achieved. Programmes are derived mainly by individual disciplines but are co-ordinated with the Project Office and Planning Department. Programming is largely dependent on the quality of the brief, particularly with regard to scope, complexity and realism of key dates throughout the project concerned. For management purposes design programmes consist of the following levels.

- 1. A global/management programme with key dates for construction and commissioning.

- 2. A project control programme for the main activities of engineering work, including information required across disciplines.
- 3. A design team programme for all the activities of analysis, design and detail — this requires the smallest practical packages of work for detail monitoring of progress.
- 4. More complex projects, or more complex aspects of design and detail which require networks to show the critical path.

Figs 4.1—4.3 show examples of programmes for working drawings, arranged to suit a practical sequence of construction for the B & C work but also to respect key access dates for installation of plant and equipment. Once a civil contractor is appointed this sequence of issue of working drawings is reviewed and adjusted if necessary to accommodate any refinements to the originally planned sequence. In the general case a 'lead in' period of eight weeks minimum is allowed for reinforced concrete work and 26 weeks for structural steelwork.

Manpower planning

Planning of design manpower relates to the type and scale of work required of the design team and the disciplines involved. This is significantly influenced by the complexity of the work, the interaction with other bodies and requirements during construction. The design team plan for W & B is made up of an in-house Project Co-ordinator and team leaders, with support from external consultants depending upon the scale of the work. The team generally relates to a form of pyramid structure to ensure adequate levels of management and engineering expertise or control, and includes staff for liaison with the Project Office and with external consultants as appropriate to the work.

Each major project has a W & B Co-ordinator to bring together the work of the Department, who in turn is supported by a Principal Officer for each discipline involved. The Principal Officer supervises directly the work of the in-house team and that of any external consultants.

Fig. 4.4 provides an outline of the relationship between the Project Manager, the W & B Co-ordinator and the B & C design team. The Structural Design Office team is given in detail to show how a project is typically subdivided in each discipline to obtain

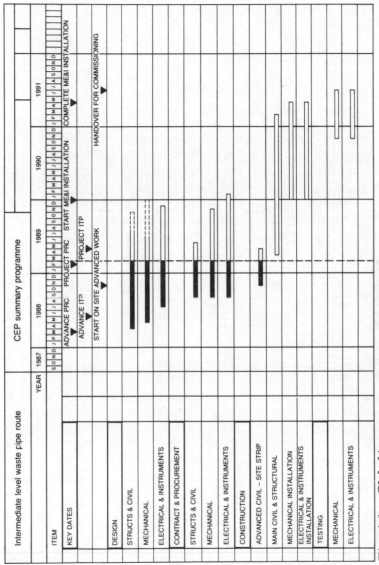

Fig. 4.1. Global/management summary programme

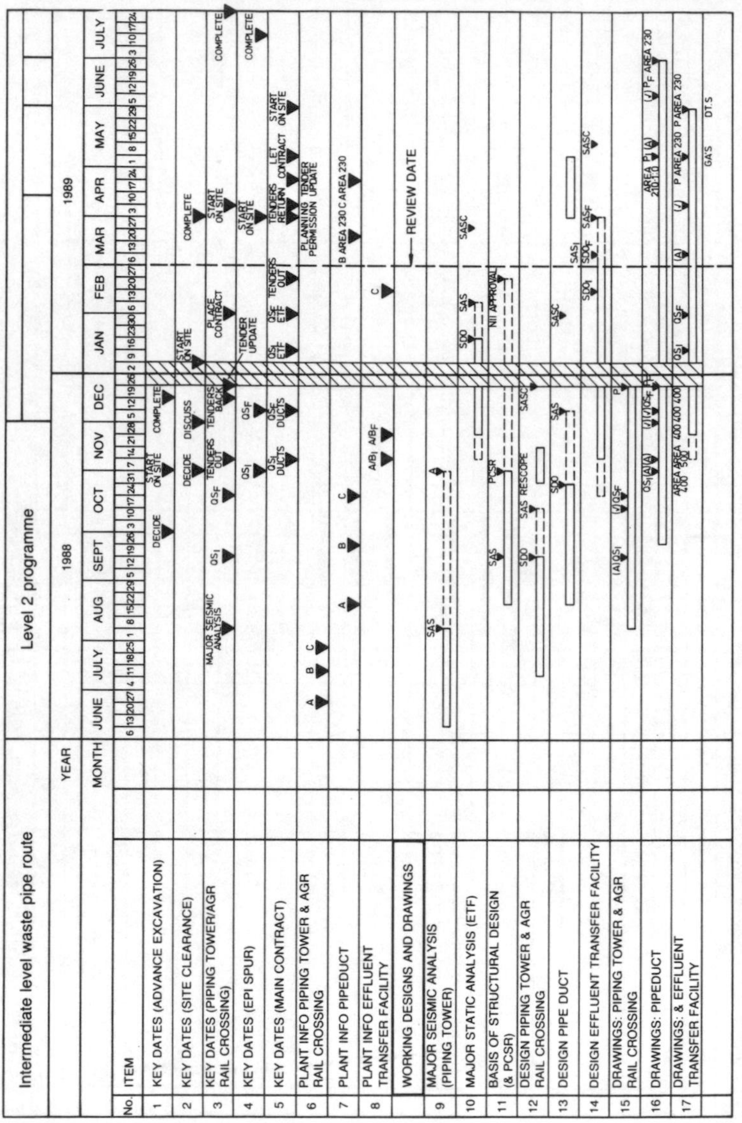

Fig. 4.2. Level 2 programme – project control

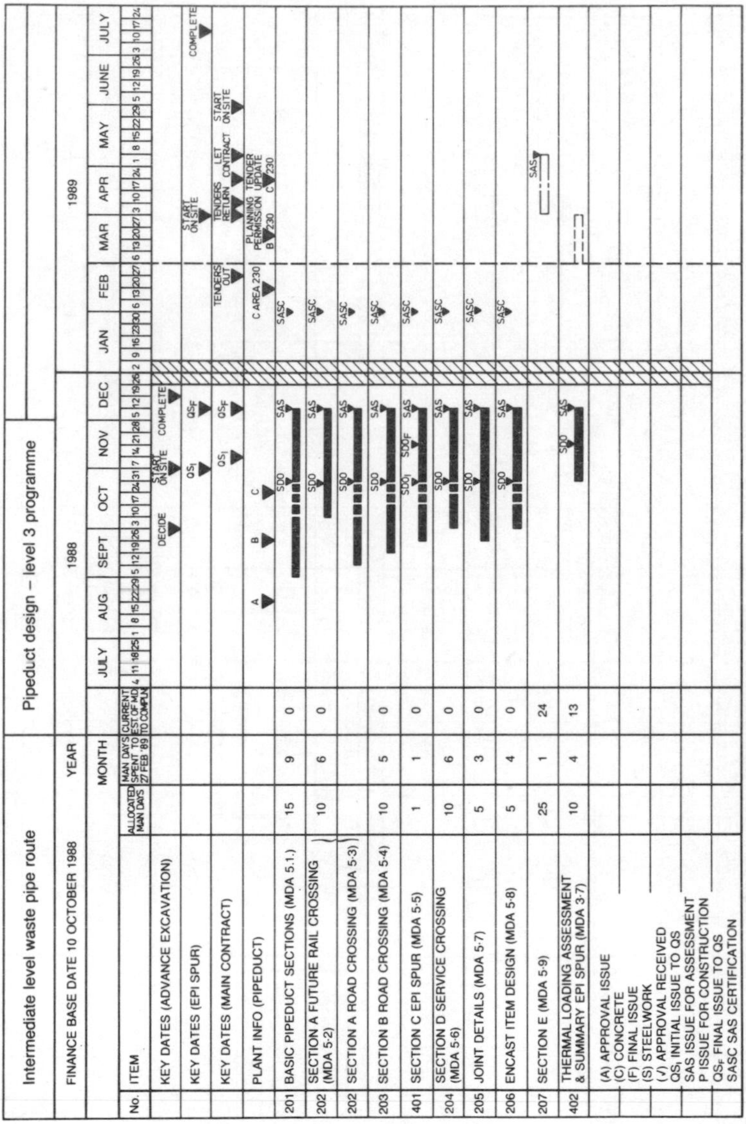

Fig. 4.3. *Level 3 programme — design*

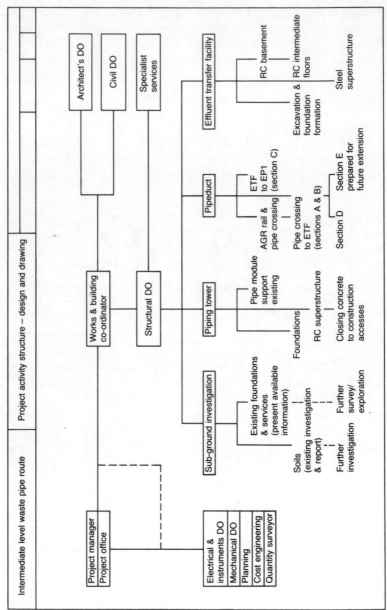

Fig. 4.4. Project activity structure — design and drawing

the appropriate level of control. The Project Office and other service offices are subdivided in a similar fashion, particularly on the larger projects.

This full team structure is combined in its efforts to control the construction costs during the design phase by reference to the cost plan as individual elements of the building and infrastructure are developed into final designs and working drawings.

Budgeting systems

The accuracy to which estimates can be made for design fund budgets requires detailed experience of the type of work involved. Any estimate is particularly sensitive to the quality of the brief in so far as a proper assessment has been made of

- the scale and scope of work
- interaction with other bodies
- the complexity of the work
- capital expenditure requirements.

Traditionally, estimates of design fund requirements are based on a percentage of the total capital expenditure of the civil engineering work. They operate best when the current project can be related to previous work. Historical data on construction costs for similar projects are used to provide estimates of capital expenditure requirements which serve to indicate both process-related and design criteria complexities as may be appropriate. These are usually expressed quantitatively in terms of the likely requirement for the amount of reinforcement per cubic metre of concrete, the weights of connections in relation to the tonnage of structural steelwork, the numbers of encast items per square metre of concrete and the requirement for stainless steel linings and their fixings − all building in comparative terms to give an indication of the total cost, for a given scope, and the complexity related thereto. These data may thus be used, with historical data on design fund expenditure, with some adjustments, to provide a budget for design work.

However, recent experience has shown that considerable care is required in the use of 'normal' percentage-based budgets on large-scale, novel or highly-engineered projects since it is not always possible to achieve the economies of scale or repetition that might be expected.

Effort is made on all projects to get commitment to the budget from staff by involving all levels of the design team, both internal and external, in making separate assessments for particular aspects of the work in which they will be involved, in either producing or supervising the design and detail. These assessments are usually based on a detailed estimate of the numbers of working drawings, allowing between 80 and 150 man-hours per drawing, depending upon scale and complexity. The effort for drawing work is then approximately doubled to allow for analysis, design and supervision. It is expected that in the general case design funds can be estimated within an accuracy of −10% to +25%, depending upon the scope and complexity of the project.

Project progress measurement

Progress measurement is made monthly, with bar line programmes covering all aspects of engineering and drawing work. Measurement of the work actually done is compared with the planned work to give a percentage of the work done against the plan, so providing an illustration of the situation at any stage. By analysis this can be extended to assess the effects of any delays on programme completion overall.

This detailed measurement of the work actually done is achieved by dividing the work into small packages for both design calculations and drawings and then monitoring each package individually before summing to give the overall achievement at any stage. The bar line programmes (see Fig. 4.3) indicate such subdivisions for both design and drawing work, and these are assessed monthly by the leader of the design team to assess the progress against the plan.

This information is used in conjunction with the project and global programmes to establish overall progress on the project. It is essential to monitor incoming information from other disciplines since this can have a significant effect on the progress of many aspects of design and detail work.

Manpower expenditure records

Manpower expenditure is recorded in detail on weekly time-sheets against each task on the design programme and, in the case of draftsmen, against drawings.

Staff at all levels are encouraged to participate in preparing programmes and making manpower assessments. In this way section leaders, designers and draftsmen are assigned a budget on which they have agreed, and which is then monitored fortnightly. Subdivisions of work on programmes (see Fig. 4.3) each have a unique number which is entered on weekly time-sheets to indicate and control the time spent for each activity. Time-sheets also identify any aspects of additional work, abortive work or delay, and particularly any time spent in making modifications to work caused by events outside the control of the design team. Only records in such detail will permit realistic monitoring of the costs.

Staff are motivated to control design changes within their discipline by their commitment and agreement to the budget for their aspect of the work. Across disciplines, motivation to limit design changes is achieved by liaison to provide

- realistic details of the information required at each stage of the design
- realistic programmes for providing information across disciplines
- proper discussion on the purpose of the information and on the repercussions of change at any stage
- realistic and helpful responses in those instances where change is absolutely necessary, and suggestions of alternative ways to reduce the impact on the design.

Cost reporting

All aspects of cost are reported monthly at design team level on the basis of

- *manpower costs:* supervision, analysis and design, drawing work, additional work/modifications, delays and abortive work and construction-related costs
- *direct charges:* computers in engineering and computers in drafting
- *indirect charges:* research and development, travel and subsistence and printing.

The cost information is reported in tabular form, giving both current monthly costs against each item and the cumulative cost from the project start date. A typical finance and resources report is presented in Fig. 4.5, which is used in conjunction with an

INTERMEDIATE LEVEL WASTE PIPE ROUTE

Finance and resources report

Period: 31 January 89–27 February 89

No. of working days: 20

Grade	Hourly rate	Total No. of men	Man days (8 h day)	Period cost	Cumulative costs from 11 Jan 88
1	25.20	1 (1)	9.81 (0)	1 978.20	
2	18.90	4 (3)	45.91 (2)	6 941.00	
3	16.25	5 (5)	94.78 (5)	12 321.44	
4	12.35	14 (15)	282.44 (14)	27 904.88	
5	9.85	12 (12)	227.53 (11)	17 929.18	
6	6.10	6 (6)	39.22 (2)	1 913.85	
Totals				68 988.55	469 461.29
Planned work total				62 688.08	318 747.48
Other work total				6 300.47	150 713.81
Non-staff activities				1 008.00	12 304.00
Total				69 996.55	481 765.29

Breakdown of costs for the period

	Planned work							Other work			
	Supervision	Engineering analysis and design	Seismic design	Drafting	Planning	Type C mods	Additional work	Work beyond level 3	NII work (Including computer)	SAS work (QA)	TQs
	6 786	14 605	0	40 950	348	4 730	1 554	16	0		0
	Printing	Computer	Travelling			Printing	Computer	Travelling	Disruption	QA	
	362	0	554			36	0	56			

Cumulative costs from 11 Jan 88

	Planned work							Other work			
	Supervision	Engineering analysis and design	Seismic design	Drafting	Planning	Type C mods	Additional work	Work beyond level 3	NII work (Including computer)	SAS work (QA)	TQs
	45 042	82 047	0	186 720	4 940	27 107	122 847	16	743		0
	Printing	Computer	Travelling			Printing	Computer	Travelling	Disruption	QA	
	2 498	1 231	4 428			1 020	115	3 012			

Fig. 4.5. *Finance and resources report*

expenditure histogram (Fig. 4.6) to provide a more pictorial representation of the actual cost in relation to that originally planned.

These same data are then used to complete a graphical representation of the projects using planned/actual work comparison curves (Fig. 4.7) and planned/actual cost comparison curves (Fig. 4.8). The curves shown in Figs 4.7 and 4.8 indicate, respectively, that work is being done according to the plan and that the expenditure to date for the volume of work planned is within the budget (the broken lines represent the actual work or actual expenditure). These two less detailed curves are used for reporting to project manager level and above.

The actual effort of completing and updating these standard forms or curves on a monthly basis is a simple matter once they have been established from the project plan. The discipline of compiling and formally reporting actual progress and expenditure against the project plan at design team level and project manager level generates a real incentive for the team to be cost-effective and to maintain programmes and budgets.

Monitoring

Monitoring of the design team progress is made monthly, covering

- progress on incoming data and design information
- progress on the engineering and detail work
- manpower availability and performance
- project costs related to planned and effective work.

The progress of incoming information is measured against a series of key dates given on the project control programme. Achievement of these dates is fundamental to the subsequent achievement of engineering progress and effective use of design resources. It is also necessary to monitor the rate of flow of incoming information, which is done by considering each element of data in relation to the standard check lists, as referred to previously. This covers such aspects as operating loads and temperatures, plant layouts and loading, encast item positions and details and stainless steel linings.

Review reporting

On major projects, progress and cost reports are reviewed on

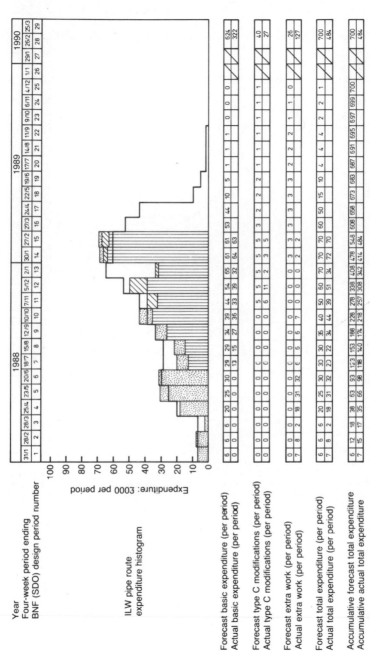

Fig. 4.6. *Expenditure histogram*

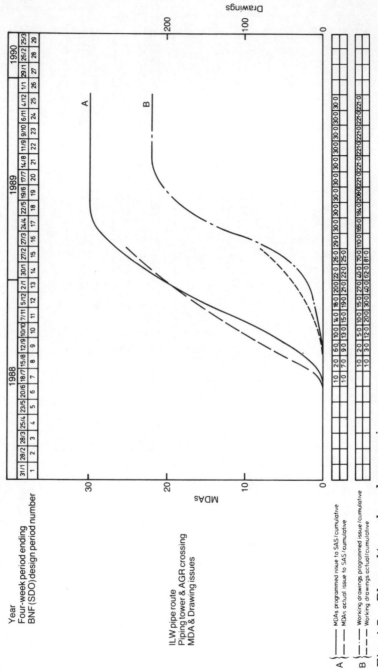

Fig. 4.7. Planned/actual work comparison curves

58

a monthly basis. The design team leader prepares, as required, summary progress reports on the project work, covering any critical areas in detail. Such reports will include a financial statement relating to actual and effective expenditure. The more senior progress reports at design team level formalize detailed progress monitoring on designs and drawings at section level, as indicated in Fig. 4.4, which are held frequently at the start of a project as concepts of the design are developed and the project plan is derived.

Result analysis

The purpose of detailed reporting is to show whether or not the design work is progressing to plan, and if not, why not. If the scope of work remains the same and the progress is satisfactory, analysis becomes simple. However, if the work is not proceeding to plan or budget, it becomes necessary to analyse

- the effects on progress of incoming design information
- the effects on progress of delays in design and detail
- the effects on other disciplines and construction
- the effects on cost regarding savings, further funding and diversity across disciplines.

Initially the W & B Co-ordinator conducts a review of the factors affecting the design or the budget, and where appropriate or practical initiates corrective action. Should a problem be indicated by lack of progress, as reflected in Fig. 4.7, or by significant differences in planned/actual expenditure, as shown in Fig. 4.8, the performances in design and drawing work are summed and superimposed on the accumulated expenditure. A sample of this procedure is given in Fig. 4.9, which shows how overspend is calculated. Underspend is determined in a similar manner.

If the problem that is developing is significant, or involves other disciplines, the W & B Co-ordinator will advise the Project Manager of the situation and agree a course of action to suit the overall needs of the project.

Yardsticks

Design team programmes are broken down into small packages of work with key dates, which make useful yardsticks for interim or global measurement of progress, trends and cost implications.

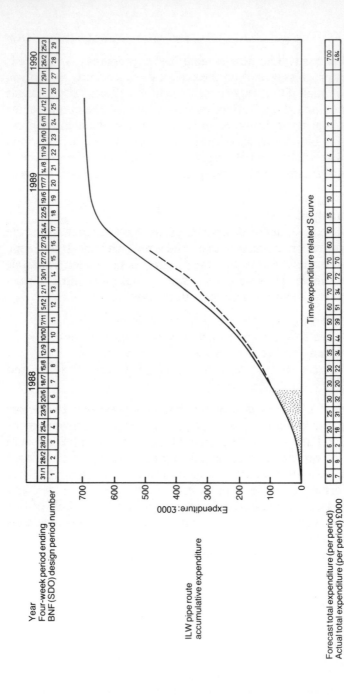

Fig. 4.8. Planned/actual cost comparison curves

60

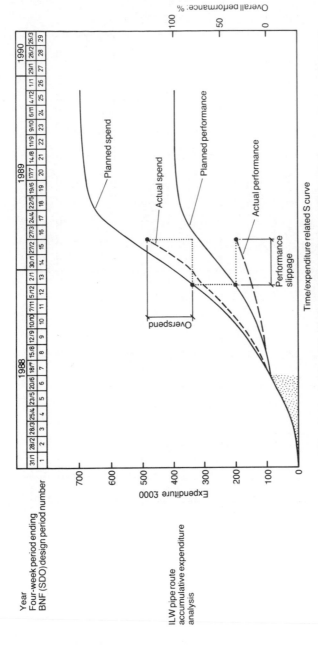

Fig. 4.9. Accumulative expenditure analysis

61

INTERMEDIATE LEVEL WASTE PIPE ROUTE

Structural drawing analysis

Base date: 2 March 89

Initial and tender drawings	Totals		In hand		Complete		Overall: %	
	Present	Previous	Present	Previous	Present	Previous	Present	Previous
Feasibility study	12	(12)	0	(0)	12	(12)	100	(100)
Initial scheme proposals	26	(26)	0	(0)	26	(26)	100	(100)
Initial proposals booster tank room	18	(18)	0	(0)	0	(0)	50	(50)
Sub-total	56	(56)	0	(0)	38	(38)		
Tender drawings AGR rail crossing	10	(10)	0	(0)	10	(10)	100	(100)
Tender drawings pipeduct	27	(27)	0	(0)	27	(27)	100	(100)
Tender drawings ETF	14	(14)	0	(0)	14	(14)	100	(100)
Sub-total	51	(51)	0	(0)	51	(51)		
Total initial drawings	107	(107)	0	(0)	89	(89)		

Working drawings									
Setting out and external works	All aspects	3	(3)	0	(0)	3	(3)	100	(100)
Piping tower & AGR rail crossing	All aspects	14	(14)	0	(0)	14	(14)	100	(100)
Pipeduct	General	15	(17)	15	(14)	0	(0)	92	(57)
Pipeduct	Section A main route	14	(13)	14	(13)	0	(0)	95	(88)
Pipeduct	Section B main route	17	(17)	17	(14)	0	(0)	90	(64)
Pipeduct	Section C EP1 spur	13	(8)	0	(0)	13	(8)	100	(100)
Pipeduct	Section D main route	6	(6)	6	(6)	0	(0)	93	(75)
Pipeduct	Section E & EP2 spur	13	(15)	9	(4)	0	(0)	45	(19)
Effluent transfer facility	Concrete GAs	28	(25)	27	(24)	0	(0)	60	(72)
Effluent transfer facility	Concrete details	43	(43)	19	(19)	0	(0)	19	(16)
Effluent transfer facility	Steel	13	(9)	10	(8)	0	(0)	38	(67)
Total working drawings		179	(170)	109	(92)	30	(25)	63	(56)

Fig. 4.10. Structural drawing analysis

A typical list of packages is given in Fig. 4.10. The yardsticks include

- key dates for incoming design information
- key dates for periods of design work
- key dates for periods for general arrangements and approvals
- periods for detail drawings.

In addition, manpower performance graphs provide an early indication of the effectiveness of the design team and allow predictions to be made regarding programme and cost.

Feedback

Detailed programming and monitoring provides feedback to management on the progress achieved, together with a statement on the cost-effectiveness of the design team. A report to management includes

- the predicted outcome of current levels of achievement, taking into account any float
- the effect of current progress on the remaining design work and on-construction activities
- any actions required to achieve acceptable levels of performance to correct any programme problems
- a financial summary covering current performance, including the effects of any corrective actions.

Feedback is imparted to design staff in-house and to external consultants by regular meetings, many at section level, when the problems of programme delays or budget overruns are discussed. All levels of the team can thus be made aware of the more global project requirements. The design team is encouraged to improve the basic project plan to increase the programmed float wherever practical, particularly in relation to construction interface.

At all stages of the B & C design the W & B Co-ordinator preserves the programme float. During the construction phase the Project Manager and the W & B Co-ordinator jointly preserve the civil construction float in conjunction with the Resident Engineer's staff, to provide maximum flexibility for unforeseen construction or contractual problems.

BNF plc considers it beneficial for designers to have feedback from the site regarding construction problems on the work they have performed. This applies to both in-house staff and external consultants. Arrangements are made for designers to visit sites at appropriate times and inspect at full scale the work they have designed, and to discuss any problems with the Resident Engineer's staff and civil contractors. In addition, designers are seconded to the Resident Engineer's staff on a selective basis to assist in the supervision of construction work.

5 A team leader's view

The management and organizational structure of a design office must reflect the nature of the design task. Large projects require large teams, which can justify the inclusion of specialists which smaller projects may not; hence the theoretical structure of a design team is often determined by project size. The project progresses through various stages − concept, preliminary design, detailed design − and will require differing levels of staff with different skills at each stage.

This chapter presents particular issues and problem areas where shared experience may be helpful. Before looking at some of these, therefore, it is useful to describe the function and role of the design office from which that experience has been obtained.

The Design Office

The Staff Office, consisting of around 45 engineering and technical staff, acts as a technical support service to project teams in other departments by providing the design and detailing of civil engineering and building structures.

The work is received by the Design Office from a project team led by a Project Engineer, based in another department, where the main discipline might be in public health, marine work etc., and is assigned by the Design Office Manager to a Job Engineer. The Job Engineer is responsible for meeting in full all the technical and programme requirements of the element of work. The Project Engineer based in the 'client' department is responsible for 'packaging' and placing the order for the work. The order is specific with regard to

- what is to be done
- what is not to be done

- when it is to be completed
- what budget in terms of man-hours has been allowed.

Usually the Job Engineer agrees these components with the Project Engineer before the order is placed. The commitment of both parties to the task enhances the chance of its successful outcome. The budget is estimated on the number of drawings required. Typically a series of small-scale free-hand drafts of each of the drawings required is made, with an estimate of time for design and drafting made against each.

The payroll costs for the preparation (i.e. designed, detailed, checked and approved) of an A1 size drawing of reinforced concrete work ranges from between £400 and £1000 (1989 costs) and depends on the complexity and the amount of reworking necessary to cope with late amendments. Experience on previous work can be used to assess fairly accurately (within 10%) the total amount of work involved.

An important consideration at the planning stage is to determine how the task might be achieved with the minimum of abortive work. Abortive work often arises by starting the design process prematurely or out of sequence. The Project Engineer has a responsibility here, and it requires a mature approach to 'hold' a project while design input parameters are being firmed up. Equally, the Project Engineer must have confidence that the design office will 'perform' when he or she does release the work, otherwise there will be a temptation to give the go-ahead prematurely. On receipt of the Project Engineer's order, the Job Engineer agrees with the Design Office Manager the staff to be deployed.

Despite the emphasis on planning, work often arrives in the office with little advance warning and usually against tight deadlines. As a result departmental priorities shift and work schedules have to be constantly revised. Against this background technical discipline has to be maintained to ensure standards and a reasonably common approach to all design problems within the firm as a whole.

Quality control
Rules covering the preparation and checking of calculations and drawings are contained in office manuals which are mandatory.

The Job Engineer is responsible for ensuring that the rules are applied. In particular the Job Engineer ensures that all appropriate standards are used and that the work is checked by an appropriately qualified and experienced engineer or technician. Any disagreement arising during checking is passed to the Design Office Manager. If necessary, the disagreement is also passed to higher management for adjudication.

Audits are carried out by the firm's quality assurance (QA) department to ensure compliance with the procedures, particularly those covering the checking of calculations, drawings, adequacy of records and storage of documents. However, QA is only an aid to sound design procedures. The most important contributor to good work is individual and group morale. If designers do not talk to one another mistakes will be made no matter how many formal checks are applied.

The view is often expressed that there is a basic conflict between quality and the desire to reduce design costs. At first glance it would seem obvious that any tendency to simplify or economize on the design process must be at the expense of the quality of the final designs. However, this is hardly ever the case in practice.

Badly-managed jobs produce bad design and high design costs. Good design arises from the design process being properly planned and then pursued enthusiastically. Good planning consists of taking time to ensure that work is done in a logical and coherent manner: logical in that each stage of the process follows on from the previous (for example data from site investigation are available in advance of foundation design); coherent in that the same approach is applied to each section of the project (for example similar loadings and standards are used). This in turn makes for economy in design costs.

Organizational climate

For any work group to be effective it should be given a single realistic task, and the people in the group should feel that the task is worth while. Can group effectiveness be established given the interruptions that must come as the necessary changes in priorities mentioned above are made and group membership is altered? Can individual motivation be sustained? Can project and quality control systems be maintained in such circumstances? The key to success in this situation lies in the creation of a positive organizational climate. The achievement of this opens the way to increased individual and group effectiveness and thus to productivity gains and improvement in design quality, reduction in problems of co-ordination and enhanced flexibility.

What is a positive organizational climate? In simple terms, it is an atmosphere of mutual trust in the office; where 'taboo' subjects are virtually non-existent; where problems are openly discussed; where staff do not attempt to shift blame to others; and where scapegoats are not sought. A particular indicator of the state of the organizational climate is the organization's capacity to learn. Are ideas and better methods of working discussed and passed on from one person to another?

The establishment of such a regime must be the principal aim of the design office managers. How do they achieve it? General theories of human relationships, leadership, group dynamics and so on are well known and thoroughly discussed elsewhere. They are all appropriate when sensibly applied. However, it is not uncommon to find managers who are strong on theory and weak in practice!

The group must be structured so that it can cope with the change in demand. It must be cohesive so that the effect of good teamwork is maximized and yet it must be flexible. A characteristic of such a group is that there is a great deal of social interaction between the members; they are loyal to one another so that the high level of interaction required between them during the design process is achieved. To construct such a group a strictly hierarchical formal structure should be avoided. To achieve flexibility senior members must be able to act comfortably in a subordinate role from time to time, and so rank must not be perceived as forever fixing the role of any individual in the team. Senior members should be able to justify their position by their ability or personality. The analogy can be made to that of the captain of a cricket team. Not necessarily the best cricketer, the captain sets the field and calls the changes but can act out a subordinate role as fielder as specialist bowlers and batsmen dominate the immediate scene.

There is a tendency when any group is under pressure for management to impose more formal and additional control in an effort to help. This should be carefully considered since the imposition of any new system from the outside on a highly-motivated cohesive group will be resented.

Environmental problems

Particular problems of a design office which affect organizational climate are as follows.

Goals

A lack of understanding of what the individual designer's goals and objectives are and communication breakdowns which lead to a misunderstanding of project requirements, particularly regarding programme, all lead to inefficiency. To avoid this all members of the office should have their workload schedule, which is planned in agreement with their immediate superior, they should know what the deadlines are and they should be responsible for meeting the deadlines.

There are various methods of analysing, scheduling and allocating work. However they are arrived at, clear-cut individual and group objectives and agreed budgets are essential. Rescheduling of work must be done sensitively to ensure that design continuity is maintained and the inevitable frustration caused by changing goals is minimized. Team leaders should not be changed during a project if at all possible.

Deadlines

In setting a workload schedule false or impossible deadlines should be avoided. Each group or individual must be wound up to meet a deadline. There is a limit to the number of times this can be done if it is believed that deadlines that have been set were not really necessary. Designers need to believe in the importance of their work. If their talents are perceived by them to be squandered, they will eventually not function efficiently and may become mere time servers or move to another organization. This effect can occur when clients change their mind, stop and restart. This is not easy to avoid, but the potential damage should be recognized. Wise understanding of the client's need is required of the project engineer to foresee such problems before they arise. In the reprogramming of the work, time allowance should be given to picking up the threads and remotivating the design team.

A further danger arising from changing deadlines is that an air of unreality creeps into the design process and carelessness occurs because it is perceived that nothing will ever be put to the test by being actually constructed. Good design is not easy to achieve, and designers need the discipline of knowing that their designs are actually going to be used.

Problem solving

Engineering problems have to be openly debated and reviewed from differing perspectives. The existence of the dogmatic know-all character in any organization dealing with complex issues and problems is dangerous. Isolation of expertise must be broken down. Experts from other groups, for example geotechnics, must be made to feel part of the team since swift and efficient interaction between all designers is a key to success. Experts should still be responsible, however, for their input through their head of discipline in their parent department.

New techniques

Technological change, like all change, can be difficult to absorb. The important point is that it probably leads in the short term to a reduction in flexibility owing to an increase in specialization and thus division within the group. This puts additional pressure on the design office manager since rescheduling and re-assignment of staff becomes more intense and complex. If change can be managed as a continuous process rather than as a series of large discrete steps it will appear less dramatic and less threatening.

The organization's rate of absorption of the new technique should ideally match its rate of introduction. This can best be achieved by ensuring that the members of the design team are taken into account in the decision making process associated with acquisition of new equipment and computer software. Again the rate at which the organization can deal with change itself depends on the organizational climate. Are members willing to teach and be taught by others? Informal group learning is very effective since, of necessity, it deals with real life issues.

Recruitment

Staff recruitment is important in establishing a proper balance and dynamic. In interviews, the capacity of the interviewee to fit into the environment is as important a question as whether he or she is a high flier. The really talented engineer is always welcome in a group which is open and motivated to doing a good job and where personal gain at others' expense has a relatively low priority.

The emphasis during recruitment must be to enrich the texture of the group.

Open-plan offices

Climate is also affected by accommodation. The best type of office for the type of organization described is open-plan. The constant rescheduling of work requires teams to form and reform rapidly. The splitting up of the office rooms can create competing groups, which reduces flexibility. Open-plan assists processes of developing mutual trust and open discussion. The team must be able to discuss their problems around the coffee machine.

Remuneration

Motivation of staff by financial reward alone is not effective in the design office since individual professional motivation comes from interest in the job and the effects of working in a good team in a supportive atmosphere. However, the view of Herzberg and others that unless financial reward is perceived to be fair it can be a most powerful demotivator is borne out in the Author's experience. This is also true of promotion where the peer group considers it unmerited.

Once discontent develops, however, it is often voiced as dissatisfaction with remuneration, and as such has to be dealt with. Dealing with the symptom does not cure the underlying problem. If company policy with regard to leave, remuneration, fringe benefits etc. is perceived simply as a measure of control for control's sake, it can be a powerful demotivator. Any policy which creates a feeling of 'them and us' is unhelpful. A proliferation of forms and memoranda imposing controls can sap the enthusiasm of any design group and can lead to a displacement of goals; i.e. it becomes more important to fill in the form than to do the work.

Formal project and quality control

The role of the manager, having created a sensible structure and a positive organizational climate, is to maintain these conditions through all the changes of demand put on the office. Here, formal project and quality control systems can reinforce and underpin the situation. Ironically, the imposition of such systems on an organization where morale is low and staff are antagonistic to management is liable to be ineffective in the short term, at least, since their success is dependent on staff co-operation. At best in such circumstances staff will merely go through the motions and the controls will become simply symbolic, or the controls will be subverted or ignored or, worst of all, they become an end in themselves and are pursued relentlessly to the exclusion of all else, including effective design.

Summary

The design office must be able to cope with changing circumstances. To do this, staff must be motivated to accept rescheduling of work and priorities, and this can only be achieved in a climate of high individual and group morale. Formal control systems may increase morale when morale is high but certainly reduce it when it is low.

6 A design organization in a large construction group

Organization of project teams

A design organization within a large construction group may be constituted in a variety of ways.

- It may be established solely to serve the group's requirements in design and construction, effectively a 'controlled' overhead with an appropriate method of accounting against tenders and contracts. The advantages may be in closeness and identity with the contracting profit centre, knowledge of its methods, aims and objectives, and specialization in its predominant field of work. Against these factors such an organization may become myopic and over-specialized, and eventually suffer from lack of scope and external stimulation.

- It may be established virtually as an independent consultancy, fully self-accounting and a profit centre in its own right and able to take (or reject) work from any source, either within or outside the group. Such an organization enjoys all the benefits to be derived from the pressures and stimulation of the market-place but must, of course, survive and be judged on the same criteria. Disadvantage to the group may arise from lack of identity with the contracting front and possibly (but not inevitably) diminished performance in design and construct contracts.

- In between these two lie many mixtures and variants. The best compromise may be a group-oriented consultancy, whose aims and objectives are closely allied to group interests, but which is able to undertake external commissions in order to broaden the base, keep in touch with the wider market and generally benefit from external influences. A high degree of, if not total, self-accountability is nowadays normally considered an essential discipline, but it is probably wise at group level to recognize that overall interests may be served by selective support for certain beneficial markets.

Whichever type of organization is chosen, it is essential to adopt a management structure which allows staff progression to be both perceived and attained. Within the structure it is desirable for staff to be able to move from one design group to another, and to be allocated different tasks to enable the office to respond to changing demands. Such movement and allocation must obviously take place within an ordered system of management, in which each member of staff is in no doubt as to whom he or she is reporting to and in which all the managers or leaders at every level are clear as to who is on their staff and how far their responsibility for those individuals extends.

In a small design office it may be sufficient and even desirable for staff to weld themselves into a team where duties and responsibilities are tacitly understood and mutually respected. Such informality has sometimes been notably effective. However, in a large office a more formal structure becomes essential, and this should be supported by written job descriptions and schedules of responsibility to cover each function and level of management. No one should be a 'floater' or a law unto himself, and although a group or section in a design office is far from being a military platoon each leader should feel that type of responsibility for and identify with his or her personnel.

At all levels, staff should be able to recognize in their immediate leaders and in senior management a real concern for them as individuals, an example in commitment to the job in hand, and a willingness to bring their own efforts and skills to bear on the day-to-day problems. In matters of management, staff loyalty is of inestimable value, but it has to be earned and nurtured.

It is a vital principle of design management that all managers should always leave a deputy to assume responsibility in their absence. Most design offices have to maintain a flexible system of grouping in order to meet fluctuating demands, but it is normal to group a number of staff, in the range of, say, 20—40 people, under the responsibility of a partner (or equivalent). The partner should seek to generate a group spirit and identity and will allocate projects and tasks to appropriate sections, which may vary widely in size according to need. It is important that, whatever the size of section, it should be led by a person of quality and experience equal to the task and made up of a balanced team. If, for example, the team is composed mainly of junior staff there may be shortcomings which cannot be avoided by effort and enthusiasm alone. It is desirable to maintain a degree of specialism where a sequence of similar projects or type of work occurs in order to maximize the efficiency and economy to be derived from repetition, but this should be balanced by work variety, particularly for those in the early stages of their career.

No management organization in a design office should be too rigid. There are those individuals who show high technical ability and preference, those who move naturally towards management of people and events while maintaining a technical base and those who perhaps shine in training. All individuals should be able to see appropriate award, progression and recognition as essential to the team effort. In responding to different types and size of project, it may occasionally be necessary for a senior member of staff to report to a junior project engineer, and this should be accepted by all staff.

Recruitment and technological change are closely related. Since the Industrial Revolution technological change has been rapid, and design offices have benefitted from the flow of new knowledge with new blood. It is, in fact, a two-way flow. A vital design office will be in the forefront of change and will both contribute to and benefit from the academic and professional fields. Recruitment should be as regular as workloads allow and selective to suit the current and anticipated workload.

Supervision and motivation of staff

The best discipline is self-discipline; the best motivation comes from within. These are truisms recognized by most organizations, particularly those composed primarily of qualified and professional staff, but to achieve that spirit of individual and team motivation which characterizes some offices is not an easy task. There is an elusive intangibility about it, often generated by one supreme personality.

Engineering is traditionally a self-motivating job. Engineers are rarely in it for the money, and, in the fine words of that great engineer Freyssinet, 'it is that realm in which fraud holds no sway'. We therefore start with good material, and those design office organizations are best which guide firmly but fairly, lead by example and somehow engender the feeling that all staff are valuable and valued contributors.

Within this general philosophy it is necessary to apply discipline, restraint and, above all, cost control. It is incumbent upon managers to set a good example and to apply as strong discipline to staff as they expect of themselves. Praise at all levels should be given generously when earned, but conversely firm discipline against slackness or lack of effort should be applied and should be expected. Staff will generally respond to and indeed welcome a tight ship if run on lines of fairness. Demotivating factors are

- over-rigid organization, for example an engineer unable to consult a colleague in another group without some protocol
- compartmentalization, for example an engineer kept on the same type of work too long
- remote leadership, for example 'we never see the boss, he's always in his office or in a meeting'
- stifled initiative, for example the bright idea ignored by bureaucratic management
- lack of recognition, for example flair and dedication going unnoticed.

It is easy to allow such factors to creep into an otherwise well-run office owing to pressure of work or complacency. The price of office vitality is vigilance combined with concern for the individual.

It is well known that in a design office analysis and calculations can get out of control, and, if unsupervised, these tasks can become almost an end in themselves, leading to excess cost. Restraint in this respect must come from experienced guidance, and junior staff should not be allowed to undertake complex analysis without a daily check on progress.

The costing system must be as accurate as possible and should produce regular feedback without delay. Nearly all offices use time-sheets, which should be subject to a management check and then fed into a computer system (which may be of varying complexity). Essentially the output should monitor project cost against target (and projected profit) and should also create as much statistical feedback as possible in order to build the office fund of cost and targeting data.

The estimation of percentage completion of projects is a vital element in any design office costing system, and is one which is often inaccurately assessed. An estimate of work remaining, rather than percentage completion, is more realistic, and for this exercise rose-tinted spectacles must be set aside. A considered estimate of excess work remaining must trigger appropriate action.

All such data then form the basis of realistic and economic targets, and the circle is complete when management exercises the discipline and control to ensure that they are achieved. The response of a team to meet targets is, again, largely a result of self-motivation; if the spirit is there the goal will usually be attained.

In the contractor's design office the design programme is intimately interlocked with procurement, approvals and construction, so at the outset of a project precise and usually demanding targets are determined.

The price of achieving quality is perpetual vigilance. Mistakes will occur, and any design office must have a checking system both for calculations and for drawings. Checking is an unenviable task, and a good checker is an extremely valuable member of staff. Checking essentials are

- self-check
- checking crucial items
- checking calculation results and conclusions rather than arithmetic
- checking co-ordination of related drawings.

Any competent engineer can undertake checking, and indeed in a busy design office most staff will be called upon to do so from time to time. There are, however, some whose natural inclinations are more apt for this task, and their skills should be utilized where possible. The skill and experience of the checker should be appropriate to the work concerned, and crucial items should be identified (and if necessary checked) at a very high level of management. The Author's organization has a standing order on checking philosophy and detail in which a key principle is self-check; i.e. the originator is duty bound to check his or her own work with sufficient care to render the work clean for the checker.

An important element in supervision and motivation of staff is the creation of a framework of actions and principles which are seen by staff as the driving force of the office with which they can identify. There is no magic formula, and indeed words without actions are of little value. It is, however, useful to summarize certain ideas and principles which can easily be assimilated and remembered. The following seven 'PCs' are suggested.

- *Personal commitment:* Without this no contribution is effective.
- *Projection to customer/client perception of 'c's requirements:* Customer satisfaction is the best recommendation. The opposite is the worst.
- *People and communications:* These are the essential ingredients which weld a team together.
- *Planning and control:* Whatever the job, nothing is achieved without strategy and control.
- *Procedures and common sense:* These are complementary. Each is essential but neither is sufficient in itself.
- *Personal checking:* Everyone should check their own work. Others should not be relied upon to pick up errors.
- *Perceived commercialism:* The balance of a commercial margin and a quality product is essential.

Staff auditing and training

In a well-organized design office, staff auditing is continuous and on several levels.

- The day-to-day project management structure should be a channel both for staff to request training and for leaders to propose training where the need is identified.
- The overall management structure should be such that all staff are known to senior managers and a regular interest taken.
- Any large design office should identify a careers manager or training officer.
- An annual review structure, formalized to some degree, should exist.
- A system of graduate experience training should be a regular feature and should include an introductory refresher course for those entering after site training.
- School leaver trainees should be recruited regularly, and should be encouraged to undertake day-release technical college training. Those trainees demonstrating the necessary ability

should be considered for a sponsored full-time CNAA degree course.

There is a wide variety of internal or external courses aimed at refreshing or extending staff knowledge or introducing a further specialization. External courses, seminars and conferences are now offered in such profusion that one could be, and indeed some people seem to be, a full-time attender. Most large organizations have a limited number of internal courses available from which most senior staff should benefit during their career and for which staff may be recommended at the annual review. On-the-job training is an important feature, and many large organizations have internal courses with an emphasis on developing the skills of the workplace. The choice has to be selective in terms of technical value, available budget and staff workload, but a design office which aspires to be abreast of technical progress must make every effort to participate.

The annual staff review, in whatever form it exists, should be an opportunity for manager and member of staff to meet quietly and discuss his or her performance, shortcomings, problems and aspirations and for certain comments and recommendations to be recorded. Such reviews should be as open as possible, and managers should not shrink from criticism as well as praise. Monitoring of performance and progress with day-to-day counselling should be more or less continuous; thus the review interview should not normally present too many shocks or surprises.

In most organizations leadership qualities have always been sought and highly valued. Managers are encouraged to identify those elements of character and personality essential to leadership and to progress the careers of likely staff. In a major contracting group the demand for good leaders is virtually unceasing, and this need is so clearly recognized that an employee is rarely held back either because that employee's manager is reluctant to release him or her or because an individual is seen to be progressing faster than some of his or her erstwhile seniors.

In a design office a further essential ingredient of leadership is technical competence, experience and professionalism. The 'boffin' type, a vital and valuable person in the design office, is usually (but not always) content to progress technically without moving into the realms of top management. Such a personality is more valuable in the technical role, and any design office which aspires to high competence and rank in its field will do well to have an adequate basis of recognition and reward for its 'boffins', who may present a rather low profile.

Top management of design therefore usually falls to those who possess the personal qualities of leadership, but in design it is wise to ensure that these are adequately supported technically at each step of the promotion ladder.

A staff review system is normally held annually for all staff in an organization except those nearing the end of their careers. An individual should be allowed to opt out of the formal review, but most staff usually see it as a useful opportunity of self-examination and exchange of views. The review should follow a printed format but no stage should be rigid, and person-to-person interviews should be conducted as openly and informally as possible. The main stages are as follows.

- 1. A personal assessment form completed by the individual is passed to that individual's direct manager.
- 2. The manager makes his or her own assessment and prepares notes for the interview, for which privacy and sufficient time is arranged.
- 3. The interview takes place, in which the individual's good and bad points are openly discussed, progress is reviewed, training needs and requests are considered and targets may be set and agreed for implementation during the following year.
- 4. The manager completes the review form, which includes a recommendation as to potential for promotion and/or transfer.
- 5. The form generally passes through a higher manager, who annotates if necessary and initials it before passing it to the responsible director.
- 6. At this stage a separate potential review is conducted at director level, supported by appropriate managers and with the specific aim of identifying those with significant leadership or other potential.
- 7. All forms are finally passed to the appropriate personnel manager, who extracts and follows up training needs and proposals. An important aspect of any review is that it should not simply be filed away. If this occurs staff will soon become disillusioned and the system will fall into disrepute. The review

81

manager should therefore make a point of following up necessary actions, continuing with counselling and monitoring any targets which have been set.

Today's economic pressures in a shrinking world are such that competition to achieve success is making demands at all levels, and new techniques are emerging to exploit all resources to the limit, not least the human resource. It is a challenge to modern management to meet demands and achieve targets while maintaining an environment in which individual qualities and needs are not submerged.

7 Computer support

In recent years, the computer has become an everyday component of many parts of the design and construction process, and anyone involved in the management of this process should understand how computers can be used most effectively. A computer can

- offer cost savings through reducing the time to do repetitive work
- carry out detailed calculations which would be tedious, costly or impractical to do by hand
- provide the facility to store, organize and interrogate large volumes of information
- improve the quality of presentation of drawings, calculations and documents.

These characteristics can be used by civil engineers both to simulate the effects of alternative design and construction choices and to integrate together many different types of project information so as to monitor the progress of a project. In addition, computerized methods of storing information make it easy to transfer information quickly and accurately between different members of the project team.

The manager of a project should understand the extent to which every stage of the project relies on the use of computers. Many of the operations carried out by computers could be done by hand, but operations that rely on the computer's processing power or storage capabilities are susceptible to computer failure or conflicting demands from other work, which could cause serious disruption to a project. To guard against equipment failures, the manager of a project should confirm that suitable procedures to copy or 'back up' all-important information are properly carried out at appropriate intervals, especially when the latest version of important data is stored only on one computer.

Computer applications
Project planning and management

In the early stages of a project, a computer can simulate the effects of alternative design and construction choices to assist in project appraisal and planning. Standard spreadsheet programs can be used to try out different costing alternatives, whereas more sophisticated project planning software can carry out a critical path analysis to highlight the most critical stages of a project.

During the design and construction phases, a computer can store, analyse and display information about many different tasks, as well as providing detailed reference information about costings and contract documents. This information can be transmitted directly between design offices and construction sites, making the same information available to every member of the design team. The utilization of materials and manpower resources can also be monitored to improve efficiency.

The successful use of computerized project management tools relies on the accuracy of the information stored in the computer, which must be up to date and checked regularly, especially when important decisions are to be based on this information.

Design assistance

Many of the computer programs used in civil engineering design help the engineer to carry out work in a more efficient or more thorough manner than could be achieved by hand. For example a program to design a structural element according to a particular code of practice will assist in the process of satisfying all of the code's requirements and then summarize how the design complies with it, for future reference.

In road design, a computer workstation operator can produce a picture showing the effect of placing a chosen road alignment across a predefined ground surface, so assisting the designer in deciding the best alignment. An additional benefit from road design programs is that many items for bills of quantities can be calculated automatically when the final alignment is chosen.

In structural analysis, the nature of the materials must be taken into account when deciding on the method of analysis to be used.

84

Steel behaves in a relatively linear and predictable fashion, but the properties of concrete vary considerably, and soil behaviour is always difficult to predict. Several analyses with modifications to the input data may be needed to investigate how sensitive the analysis is to variations in specific input variables or to predict the consequences of any failure, and the intended sequence of construction should be checked for design cases which are more critical than those of the completed structure. When finite-element analysis is used, the size and type of elements used can greatly affect the time taken to prepare and process the analysis, and the wrong choice can lead to inappropriate results.

Network analysis provides a powerful tool to analyse water distribution systems and transportation planning models, but the apparent accuracy of the results can disguise a great deal of uncertainty which may exist in the input data.

The designer should always be aware that, although the mathematical model can be precisely analysed in great detail, the accuracy of the results is only useful if a true model of the physical situation has been created. In many cases specialist expertise will be required to obtain the best analysis, and the manager of a project must have sufficient knowledge of how the analysis is being carried out to make sure that it is cost-effective. The fact that a computer is capable of carrying out very detailed mathematical analyses does not necessarily mean that it is meaningful to do so.

Computer-aided drafting

The successful use of a computer for drafting purposes requires careful planning and management. The cost of the computer hardware, workstations, software and staff training involved in setting up a drafting system can only be justified by a considerable increase in the productivity of each member of staff involved. The difference in drawing speed between computer and hand drafting depends very much on the type of work. Whenever a significant proportion of a drawing can be copied or repeated, computer drafting will be much faster, but where a great deal of thought is required during the creation of a drawing the time taken by hand will probably be similar to that taken using a computer.

The number of drawings that can be produced on a computer in a given time is limited by the number of workstations and operators available, and by the capacity of the plotter. The production of design calculations and the effect of any major design revisions should be monitored continuously to prevent a bottleneck occurring in the drawing production process. In programming the project activities, suitable allowances should be made for the delay which could be caused by a breakdown of the plotting equipment if alternative plotting facilities are not available.

Word processing

Word processors can be used to assemble and format any type of text document, and the advantages of such systems for sending letters and preparing reports are well established. A particular area of application in civil engineering is in the preparation of contract documents such as specifications and bills of quantities, where a library of standard clauses can be assembled in appropriate combinations to form different contract documents.

Administrative functions

Every design office requires many routine administrative tasks to be carried out in an accurate and efficient manner. A computer can keep accounts, print bills and provide accurate up-to-date financial summaries whenever required. Computer-based drawing and document registers can also be used to record the completion, issue and revision of important documents.

In an integrated project management system, the administrative data can be extracted in summarized form for management analysis, and the resulting information can then be fed directly to word processing and graphic output software so as to produce reports.

Verification and checking

The designer must have complete confidence in the results of computer analysis in order to take responsibility for the project design. Whatever the source of any computer software, the designer should be satisfied that sufficient proof of the correct operation of the program has been provided. It is important that the responsibility for the computerized aspects of the design process is not delegated to junior staff merely because of their familiarity with the computer systems being used.

The many variations of input parameters to most computer programs can make thorough verification of all aspects of a program's operation a very difficult task, and it should always be quite clear who is responsible for making sure that it is carried out. The verification process must also be repeated whenever changes are made to the software. With purchased software, the need for independent verification should be considered.

All the input data to analysis programs should be checked using similar procedures to those needed for hand design calculations. For certain types of analysis, graphical displays or plotted output can be used to speed up some parts of the checking process. When very detailed or complex analysis is used, an overall rough check of the global design results using an alternative method of analysis should also be carried out to guard against conceptual errors in the computer analysis employed.

Information handling
Input and output data

The efficiency with which data are transferred to and from a computer can be an important factor in assessing the benefit gained from using it. The method used to input any data should aim to enter the data in the simplest and most easily understood form with the minimum of repetition. Wherever possible, data should be transferred directly into a computer in digital form (for example survey data), but, if data are not available in this form, with the aid of digitizing equipment the information shown on an accurate map or a drawing can be transferred directly to a computer.

The output from a program should be in the final form in which the information is required. For instance, results can be printed on A4 sheets of paper complete with headings and references for inclusion straight into calculations, and graphical output can be processed into pages for reports and then printed or plotted directly as finished pages. It should be noted that colour plotted output cannot be photocopied easily, and well-planned single-colour output is more often appropriate.

Databases and information storage

An important objective of any data storage system should be to ensure that only one up-to-date copy of each item of data is available, so that where there are multiple users everybody is always using the latest information. This involves a detailed and often specialized analysis of the data to be stored and procedures for updating it to arrive at the optimum standardized method of storage. The efficient storage and manipulation of any large amount of data is a major analysis and management task in itself.

Commercial databases can offer many benefits in organizing and managing information, and the differences between the many alternatives available merit a thorough investigation before a choice is made.

Transfer of computerized information

The direct movement of computerized data from one stage of the design process to another saves time and reduces errors. The amount and type of data to be transferred between the different members of a design team should be assessed in the early stages of a project. As an example, computerized drawings can be transferred between different offices, but the information requirements of architects, engineers and services engineers are all different and they are likely to use different computer systems. Drawings will probably be updated frequently during design, and so the transfer of data is likely to be on a regular basis. Standardized methods of transfer can be developed, but sometimes these prove inefficient for large volumes of data unless special software is created to manage the transfer task.

Training and motivation

The training required to use a computer program will depend on both the type of application and on the computer literacy of the users. Interactive programs which ask the user a series of questions and provide detailed descriptions of the input required are very useful for the occasional user when only a small amount of data is required, but where large amounts of data need to be input on a regular basis the simplest form of input is required with the minimum of explanation. So-called user-friendly programs which may appear to be very easy to use because of their extensive dialogue may actually be very frustrating to the regular user who knows all the questions and answers off by heart and would rather have a system of default values and simplified codes for standard sets of answers.

In general, technical users will readily learn standardized methods of working to improve their daily throughput of work and will benefit from well-directed training courses, whereas management users require many different types of data on an occasional basis and will prefer self-explanatory interactive programs with comprehensive help facilities.

Rapid advances in computer technology have led to complementary changes in the skills required of the staff that work with computers. Organized training and well-defined working procedures can assist in introducing such changes into the office and maintaining morale among workstation operators.

Sources of computer software
In-house program development

The cost of developing in-house software can be extremely difficult to estimate. Any such costing exercise should include the time spent preparing a software specification, an estimate of the time to write the software and additional time for program verification and testing. When software is developed, the possible re-use of the software for other projects and any future marketing potential to other organizations should be taken into account as this represents a possible offset in the development costs.

Documentation of the software itself can be a useful method of monitoring the progress of software development as well as providing vital information for the future maintenance or extension of the program. As far as possible, all the knowledge about how a program works should be in a form that can be located and understood by another programmer, rather than relying on the expertise of particular individuals.

Commercial software

The difficulty of selecting the most appropriate commercial software for a specific purpose should not be underestimated. More expensive software will often offer long-term benefits, and the assessment of each alternative should involve staff with sufficient technical and managerial knowledge to take all the implications of implementing any new system into account.

Commercial software can offer a standardized solution with good technical support and continuous development to suit changes in design standards and methods. These benefits may often outweigh the fact that the software does not offer the ideal solution to every task. User groups organized in conjunction with software suppliers provide an important forum to exchange ideas and feed back comments on many major commercial systems.

Computer installations
Centralization of computer facilities

A centralized system can offer the means of sharing expensive facilities between a large number of occasional users, so that each user can effectively have access to very powerful or sophisticated facilities for short periods of time. The main benefits from using a larger computer are

- the ability to carry out more complex analysis
- common access to programs and data
- centralized computer operations and back-up.

The centralized system is more appropriate for a large organization which has the need to provide many users with access to common data or which requires a wide range of software to be available to different departments or offices.

Microcomputers

Microcomputers can be managed and operated as independent units. When computer activities can be subdivided into independent tasks, microcomputers can provide a cost-effective solution, but where the same programs are needed on every microcomputer multiple licences for commercial software can be expensive, and if the same data are duplicated on several machines they must always be updated in an organized manner. When a number of microcomputers are in use, some form of centralized support and co-ordination is recommended.

Distributed computing and networks

The latest developments in networking together computers of all sizes and types offer many new possibilities for computer installations. The complexity of such systems requires careful technical assessment when equipment is chosen, and thorough management when in operation, but the ease with which new components can be added and existing components replaced should lead to very adaptable computer systems in the future.

Management of computer facilities
Project management responsibilities

The manager of a project using a computer must be satisfied that any computerized work will be carried out accurately, efficiently and within the required deadlines. To assist in achieving this, estimates of the computer requirements for a project in terms of equipment utilization and personnel should be prepared for co-ordination with the demands from other projects. Long-term requirements for archiving and storing any computerized data should also be identified as early as possible. It should be remembered that magnetic computer tapes have a limited lifetime of only a few years and must be re-copied before they deteriorate. For long-term storage a paper print-out of important data should also be archived.

Computer management, operations and maintenance

Conflicting requirements for computer facilities must be identified and resolved by the computer manager. Routine maintenance and any repairs that may become necessary should also be managed independently of the pressures of project deadlines as far as possible.

It is important that responsibilities and procedures for backing up data are clearly defined. A large centralized system should have full-time operational staff who are responsible for carrying out such tasks according to carefully planned procedures, whereas individual users of similar microcomputer-based systems must be responsible for their own procedures. Unfortunately, it is far too easy to forget to back up vital data at a critical stage in a design, especially when it may not appear to offer any benefits to the designer until the importance of lost material is realized, often too late. When defining the back-up procedures for a computer, it should always be borne in mind how long it would take to re-create all the data which could be lost. For minor design work, a print-out of the input data may be sufficient back-up, since the data could be re-entered in only a few minutes if a failure occurs.

The computer management must also plan for future computer requirements, and should have access to technical staff who can assess and advise on alternatives. Continuous changes in workload and applications make long-term planning and co-ordination very difficult, and decisions based on the benefits for individual projects may not give the best overall return on investment.

Security

It is difficult to maintain complete security of information on a computer system. A balance must normally be struck between ease of access and security. The standard password system cannot be relied on to achieve total security. Terminals are often left logged in, allowing unauthorized access to programs and data. If security is very important, controls on personnel access to the terminal locations should be introduced and maintained. Any type of network or dial-up link can be a particular weakness, allowing invisible access from outside a secure office.

Future developments

Computer storage and processing power will continue to increase while the cost of purchasing computer hardware decreases, and in some cases the software to run on a computer can already cost more than the computer itself.

The developing science of information technology, concerned with the storage and processing of all forms of information, will have particular impact on the design office. As the computerization of the design process changes from a number of separate design programs with independent input and output into a series of design stages with information transferred directly from one stage to the next via the computer, the application of this new science is likely to become far more important.

New approaches to software design, and the realization of the importance of an efficient human interface between the computer and its users should lead to continual improvements in the software available to assist all branches of the civil engineering profession.

Sources of further information

Books on all aspects of the application of computers in civil engineering

Thomas Telford Ltd
Thomas Telford House
1 Heron Quay
London E14 9XF

Tel. 071-987 6999

Advice, reports and publications on the use of computers in construction

The Construction Industry Computing Association
Guildhall Place
Cambridge
CB2 3QQ

Tel. 0223 311246

Advice, reports and books on all matters related to computers

The National Computing Centre Ltd
Oxford Road
Manchester
M1 7ED

Tel. 061-228 6333

References

1. *New civil engineer consultants file 1989.* Thomas Telford, London, 1989.
2. Wearne S. H. *Principles of engineering organization.* Arnold, London, 1973.
3. British Standards Institution. *Construction drawing practice.* BSI, London, BS 1192.
4. Institution of Civil Engineers. *Professional liability.* Thomas Telford, London, 1988.
5. British Standards Institution. BSI, London, BS 5750.
6. British Standards Institution. *BSI standards catalogue.* BSI, London.

Bibliography

Bartle P. R. and Thorburn S. A strategic view of the European Community in the context of civil engineering codes and standards. *Mun. Engr*, 1988, Dec., 281–290.

Brearly A. *The management of drawing and design*. Gower, London, 1975.

Bronikowski R. J. *Managing the engineering design function*. Van Nostrand Rheinhold, New York, 1986.

Davis C. and Cochrane S. R. The simulation of manpower requirements for consulting civil engineers. *Proc. Instn Civ. Engrs*, 1987, **82**, Part 1, Aug., 815–829.

Engineering Council. *The Consumer Protection Act*. Engineering Council, London, 1987.

Institution of Civil Engineers. *Civil engineering procedure*. Thomas Telford, London, 1986, 4th edn.

Handy C. B. *Understanding organisations*. Penguin, London, 1986, 3rd edn.

Martin A. S. and Grover F. (Eds) *Managing people*. Thomas Telford, London, 1988.

Neale R. H. and Neale D. E. *Construction planning*. Thomas Telford, London, 1989.

Power R. D. *Quality assurance in civil engineering*. Construction Industry Research and Information Association, London, 1985.

Rogers D. N. Design in the private sector. *Mun. Engr*, 1988, Dec., 319–322.

Wearne S. H. The development of project engineers. *Int. J. Project Manag.*, 1985, Aug.

Wearne S. H. (Ed.) *Control of engineering projects*. Thomas Telford, London, 1989.

Wearne S. H. and Miller R. J. *Da Vinci, Lock & Partners, consulting engineers — an organisation for discussion*. University of Bradford, 1976, Report TMP 21.

Biographies

P. F. Buckthorp, *CEng, MIStructE, ACIArb*
Peter Buckthorp is a founder Senior Partner of Buro Happold
Consulting Engineers, and is responsible for the managment and
co-ordination of the business of this partnership. He has worked
extensively in the UK and overseas and has acquired specialist
experience in matters of banking, insurance, tax and related matters
of accountancy and business administration. The business suite
of computer programs managing the affairs of Buro Happold was
written by Peter Buckthorp, and comprises a fully integrated suite
of ledger, invoicing, time costing, job records and PAYE programs.
   His interest in engineering tends towards commercial and social
buildings. He represents the Institution of Structural Engineers
on, and is a member of the special task force investigating, PI
insurance. He is also a member of the British Standards Code
Committee in Malta. He is one of the representatives of IABSE
for Commission 5 – Construction Management 2.

J. W. Dowling, *ARIBA*
Jack Dowling, now retired, was formerly the Head of the Works
and Buildings Department of British Nuclear Fuels plc. The
Department, a branch of the Engineering Division, comprised an
integrated 200-strong team of architects, civil and structural
engineers.

A. S. Martin, *MSc, CEng, FICE, FIHT, FBIM*
Until taking early retirement in 1985, Stanley Martin had been
a Chief Officer for some 30 years, serving three local authorities,
culminating in the post of Director of Technical Services of Erewash
Borough Council, where he was responsible for engineering,

96

architecture, town planning and recreation. He has been active in the affairs of several institutions and associations, both locally and nationally, over many years, and was President of the Association of Chief Technical Officers, Chairman of the Association of Public Service Professional Engineers and Chairman of the Federation of Professional Officers Associations, as well as Chairman of the Membership Committee of the Institution of Municipal Engineers.

A keen student of management, he was awarded the degree of MSc by Loughborough University of Technology for research into aspects of municipal engineering management. He has written over 100 data sheets on management, the first 79 being published in *Can you manage?* (Municipal Publications, 1981), and is co-editor of *Managing people* (Thomas Telford, 1988).

He is Chairman of the Panel of Examiners for the Institution of Civil Engineers' examination in management and public administration, and is a member of the Association of Municipal Engineers' Affairs and Editorial Committees. He is a Freeman of the City of London.

L. W. Oliver, *CEng, MICE, MBIM*

Lawrence Oliver is a Principal Engineer with Sir William Halcrow & Partners Ltd in the company's Burderop Park office near Swindon. His engineering background is in thermal and hydro-electric power development. He has particular interest in the areas of heavy foundations, marine and tunnel work, reinforced concrete and steel structures. Over the last few years he has been Head of the Design Department of Halcrow's Technical Services Division, which deals with the design and preparation of drawings for civil engineering and building structures. He is responsible for the Department's output and general management.

A. S. Parker, *MSc, CEng, FICE*

Alan Parker took a BSc in civil engineering at Leeds University in 1950 and went on to obtain an MSc in prestressed concrete composite construction under Professor R. H. Evans. After a period of design in structural steel he joined James Williamson and Partners and worked on site on hydro-electric projects in northern Scotland. He joined John Laing's Design Department in 1956. In 1964 he was appointed one of several Associates with general responsibility for the civil/structural design office activities. Prior to his retirement in December 1986 he was Director of Laing Design Services, with overall responsibility for a multi-discipline design team of some 150 staff at Mill Hill Head Office and in branch offices.

Elected Fellow of the Institution of Civil Engineers in 1969, he has presented technical papers and has undertaken research projects while maintaining a primary interest in management organization and training.

P. A. Rutter, *MSc, DIC, CEng, FICE, FIStructE, MConsE*
Peter Rutter has been with consulting engineers Scott Wilson Kirkpatrick since 1957 and a Partner since 1981. The early years were spent on the design of concrete and steelwork structures for buildings, bridges and aircraft hangars. In 1976, after a postgraduate year at Imperial College, he returned to take charge of the civil and structural design for Heathrow Terminal 4. Subsequent projects included a military project for British Aerospace and the extension of Bahrain International Airport Terminal. A City University postgraduate diploma in management for the construction industry was obtained in 1984.

He is now Partner responsible for the London office, which undertakes, principally, structural engineering projects, and he has also a responsibility for offices in Plymouth and Basildon. He was responsible for directing the development of the GIPSYS CAD system. He was the Partner responsible for the introduction of the firm's quality assurance system and is the QA Director. He serves on various technical committees, including the BSI committee for structural steelwork design and composite design.

S. P. R. Vincent, *MA, MSc, CEng, MICE, MIStructE, MBCS*
Stephen Vincent has been with Scott Wilson Kirkpatrick since completing a general degree in engineering at Cambridge in 1977. His engineering experience ranges from rock-fill dams to multi-storey office structures, and he has retained a continuous interest in the application of appropriate computerized methods to all aspects of civil engineering throughout his career.

As well as supervising engineering design and site construction, he has studied software design methods and managed information systems development. He is currently applying the latest management techniques and computer technology to a variety of civil engineering projects.